COUSCOUS

COUSCOUS

FRESH AND FLAVORFUL CONTEMPORARY RECIPES

BY KITTY MORSE

PHOTOGRAPHS BY ALISON MIKSCH

CHRONICLE BOOKS

SAN FRANCISCO

Text copyright © 2000 by Kitty Morse
Photographs copyright © 2000 by Alison Miksch

Library of Congress Cataloging-in-Publication Data available.

ISBN 0-8118-2401-2

Printed in Hong Kong

Prop styling by Barbara Fritz
Food styling by Bettina Fisher
Designed by Ph.D
Typeset in Filosophia and Tarzana

Distributed in Canada by Raincoast Books
8680 Cambie Street
Vancouver, British Columbia V6P 6M9

10 9 8 7 6 5 4 3 2 1

Chronicle Books
85 Second Street
San Francisco, California 94105

www.chroniclebooks.com

"A North African stayed with me and fell sick," recalled a fourteenth-century Syrian sheik, "and the sickness lasted so long that I prayed to God to comfort both him and me with either death or health. In a dream, I saw the Prophet, prayers and peace be upon him, and he said, 'Feed him *al-kuskusun* [sic]' . . . I made it for him, and it was as if I had made him a cure."

FROM *Nafh al-Tib min Ghusn al-Andalus al-Ratib*
(*"The Breath of Scent from the Succulent Branch of Al-Andalus"*)
BY Ahmad Muhammad al-Maqqari al-Tilimsani (1574—1632).
TRANSLATION BY Charles Perry

acknowledgments

I am indebted to many people for assisting me in this project. I want to especially thank cookbook author and scholar Clifford Wright, and noted food historian Charles Perry, staff writer for the *Los Angeles Times*, both founts of information on the subject of couscous. My thanks to edible plant expert and author Stephen Facciola. I would also like to acknowledge the creative assistance of Froukje and Jim Frost.

My appreciation goes to friends and colleagues Nacira Baba Ahmed, Genevieve Béké, Carole Bloom, Dalia Carmel, Rivka Casey, and Grace Kirschenbaum.

In Morocco, my research was made easier thanks to the assistance of Aziz and Nadia Belkasmi, Amy Fishburn, Ahlam and Abdel Illah Lemseffer, Danielle and Jacques Mamane, Bouchaib Marzouk, Roseline and Abderrahmane Rahoule, and Susan Searight. My gratitude extends to Mohamed Jamal Eddine of TRIA, and Moulay Abderrahman Laghrari of SOCOTEN, couscous manufacturers in Casablanca and Marrakech, respectively.

I also want to acknowledge the invaluable input of family and friends, especially that of my chief taste tester and editor, my husband, Owen.

It has been a pleasure to work once again with my agent, Julie Castiglia, and with the creative team at Chronicle Books—my editors, Bill LeBlond and Stephanie Rosenbaum, and photographer Alison Miksch.

Thank you all for being so enthusiastic about **COUSCOUS**!

table of contents

INTRODUCTION

Couscous was virtually unknown in the United States in 1964, the year I arrived from my native city of Casablanca, Morocco, to begin university studies in Wisconsin. I remember the thrill of exploring an American supermarket for the first time. Never had I seen such a variety of foods on display under one roof. They seemed to have everything—everything, that is, except couscous, my favorite comfort food. The store manager had never even heard of the durum wheat semolina product, *the* staple of the Moroccan and North African diet. Fortunately, my grandfather, who also had emigrated to the United States, was able to track down a sympathetic importer in New York City who agreed to ship it to our family by the case.

How things have changed in thirty-five years! Articles about couscous appear regularly in major newspapers and national food magazines. A growing number of American companies now market couscous products in virtually every health food store in the country, as well as in most supermarkets. Its burgeoning popularity was highlighted when recipes featuring couscous won both first and second prize in the 1997 Pillsbury Bake-Off!

What pasta is to Italians, what rice is to the Chinese, couscous is to the inhabitants of the *Maghreb al-Akhsa* ("the land where the sun sets"), as the countries of Morocco, Algeria, and Tunisia are known collectively. In this part of the world, it is not unusual for families to gather around a steaming platter of couscous, topped with vegetables, meat, and broth, at least once a week.

Most scholars credit North Africa's indigenous Berbers with the invention of couscous, called *seksoo* or *ta'am* in their dialects. *Ta'am* is also their term for "nourishment," indicating the importance it has in their diet. Former Tunisian president Habib Bourghiba allegedly once said that couscous is the common thread linking the nations of the Maghreb. In other words, North Africa ends at the point where couscous gives way to rice and millet. This unofficial boundary is thought to lie somewhere west of Lybia's Gulf of Sidra.

Wheat, the cereal grain from which most couscous is made, has been an essential part of the Mediterranean diet since time immemorial. It is one of the world's oldest cultivated edible plants. Ethnobotanists have discovered evidence of wheat production at a 9,000-year-old site near Jericho, one of the world's most ancient cities.

During classical times, vast private estates called *latifundia* produced such enormous quantities of soft wheat *(Triticum aestivum)* in the Roman provinces of North Africa that the region became known as "the breadbasket of Rome." The cultivation of the more versatile durum (hard) wheat, also called "winter wheat"*(Triticum turgidum var. durum)*, did not begin in North Africa until relatively late, sometime during the period of the Arab conquest, 632 to 732 C.E.

Durum wheat is the hardest form of wheat, a property attributed to its relatively low starch and high protein content. This makes it well suited to the production of couscous and dried pasta.

In more isolated areas of North Africa, the husked grain is still crushed by means of hand-turned millstones, called *ra'ha* in Arabic. Crushing breaks up the wheat kernels into small starch granules, and into larger particles composed of protein and starch. This, the coarsest milling product, is called "semolina."

Couscous may have evolved from what the Romans called *puls*, or gruel, by way of primitive, beadlike pasta. Unlike pasta, however, couscous does not require kneading. It is not dependent upon gluten, the elastic protein that is released when a semolina-water mixture is kneaded. Indeed, several nonglutinous cereal grains, such as barley, corn, millet, sorghum, and rice, are commonly used to prepare couscous.

The fourteenth-century Arab explorer Ibn Battuta described millet and rice couscous in the region of West Africa known today as Mauritania and Mali. Morocco's Sephardic Jews still make a couscous with bread crumbs, a practice that was also common to the thirteenth-century Spanish Moors. And in São Paulo, Brazil, sixteenth-century traders from the Portuguese colonies of Africa's northwest coast introduced a couscous, now called *cuscuz Paulista*, which made use of the locally plentiful corn semolina.

The word "couscous" refers both to the dry durum wheat semolina product (although semolina from other cereal grains are also used), as well as to the popular prepared dish in which it is the principal ingredient. Food historian Clifford Wright, author of *A Mediterranean Feast: The Story of the Birth of the Celebrated Cuisines of the Mediterranean from the Merchants of Venice to the Barbary Corsairs*, believes the word "couscous" may derive from the Berber language. Other scholars think it comes from the classical Arabic word *kaskasa*, meaning "to grind." Still others theorize that it may be onomatopoetic, an imitation for the rushing, soft rattling sound that couscous granules make as they are being rolled and formed under the hand.

Whatever its etymology, couscous has been a staple of the North African diet for centuries, even though the exact date of semolina's transformation into couscous, by means of wetting and rolling, is a mystery, as is the history of the discovery that unkneaded semolina (lacking the elasticity of gluten) turned light and fluffy when steamed.

Scholars like Wright, as well as Charles Perry, a respected Arabist and a staff writer for the *Los Angeles Times*, believe that couscous first appeared sometime between the eleventh and thirteenth centuries in North Africa or Moorish Spain. According to Wright, however, there is also some circumstantial evidence pointing to the tenth-century sub-Saharan region of modern-day Mali as the birthplace of the steaming process that characterizes the making of couscous. Many North African researchers, such as Moroccan economist Naima Lakhal, in her Ph.D. dissertation, *La production et la consommation du couscous au Maroc* ("The Production and Consumption of Couscous in Morocco"), embrace the theory of Berber origination.

The thirteenth-century Andalusian author Ibn Razin Al-Tudjibi-Al-Andalusi describes the preparation of couscous in his cookbook *Fudalat al-Khiwan fi Tayibat at-Taam wa al alwan:* "After sprinkling the semolina with lightly salted water . . . you rub it gently between the palms of your hands until the semolina becomes the size of ants' heads."

For the peripatetic sixteenth-century Arab geographer Hassan-al-Wazzan, who later adopted the Latin name Leo Africanus, couscous was the ideal staple "because it costs little and nourishes a lot."

Three hundred years later, the French author Pierre Loti writes in his book *Morocco:* "The pièce de résistance of a Moorish dinner, [is] the dish of *kesk'soo* [sic] . . . *Kesk'soo* is a small round granule prepared from semolina, which, having been steamed, is served like rice beneath and around an excellent stew, which is heaped in the center of the dish. With the thumb and the first two fingers of the right hand you are expected to secure some succulent morsel from the stew—meat, raisins, onions, or vegetable marrow—and with it a small quantity of *kesk'soo*. By a skilful [sic] motion of the palm, the whole is formed into a round ball, which is thrown with a graceful curve of the hand and wrist into the mouth."

Many agrarian families in North Africa sow their own hard winter wheat in the late fall. It grows to a small plant during the Maghreb's moderately dry winter before flowering in the spring, for late spring or early summer harvest. Some urban families, compelled by tradition and economics, prefer to purchase sacks of whole grain. They, like their rural cousins, take it to the local miller's to be ground into semolina.

After the wheat is milled, women spend long hours preparing their family's supply of couscous in a time-honored process that is tedious yet deeply satisfying. They begin by placing several handfuls of semolina into a large earthenware platter called a *ga'saa*. They sprinkle the semolina with lightly salted water, and, in some regions, small quantities of hard or soft wheat flour, which bonds to the nucleus of semolina. The salinated, starch-rich coating makes the granules more resistant to oxidation and spoilage—an important quality for any staple, especially in regions where refrigeration is unavailable.

After the salted water and optional flour are added to the semolina, North African women roll the mixture with their fingers and palms, in alternating figure-eight and circular patterns, until the hard, minuscule semolina particles agglomerate into small, spherical pellets, ranging in size from peas to garbanzo beans. With their hands, they work the pellets through a series of screened sieves to produce a gradation of large, medium, and fine granules.

The coarsest (*m'hammsa*), the size of peppercorns, are used primarily for thickening soup. The medium-size granules, the variety sold in the United States, have an all-purpose application, while the tiniest ones (*s'ffa*) are those Ibn Razin described as being the size of "ants' heads." They are reserved for special occasions, and for the making of sweet couscous.

After rolling, couscous can be cooked and consumed immediately, or spread out on sheets to dry, and then stored in sealed containers. One summer, in the mid-1970s, while staying in Morocco, I rolled and dried over twenty kilos (forty-four pounds) of couscous in this manner. My supply lasted for almost five years. Even in the last cup, there was no hint of rancidity.

With increasing numbers of women working outside the home, sales of commercially manufactured couscous have exploded. To keep up with demand, modern companies such as TRIA of Casablanca must steadily increase production in their large, computerized plants. Ironically, 70 percent of the durum wheat required for the Moroccan market must be imported from the United States, Canada, and Argentina, explains Mohamed Jamal Eddine, TRIA's president, his voice barely audible over the din of enormous rotating drums, hissing steamers, massive dryers, and automated sifting machines. TRIA manufactures presteamed couscous, similar to the kind available in the United States. The process of presteaming greatly reduces final cooking time. Fifteen minutes after adding this couscous to boiling liquid, it is ready to serve.

Most North African cuisinières still employ the time-honored steaming method for cooking their couscous—some, because the presteamed variety is unavailable to them, and others, simply out of sense of tradition. This reluctance to adopt the newer method is understandable.

Couscous is more than simply food to the people of the Maghreb. It has important spiritual significance, as well. Couscous is a symbol of happiness and abundance. North Africans believe it brings God's blessing, or *barakah*, upon those who eat it. For this reason, its preparation is de rigueur on religious occasions such as the traditional midday meal on Friday, the Moslem day of rest. Pilgrims returning from the *hajj* to Mecca are treated to *k'seksoo b'il beid wa looz* (couscous with eggs and almonds), a dish crowned with caramelized onions and raisins, lightly scented with saffron and cinnamon, and garnished with hard-boiled eggs to symbolize purification and renewal. Couscous is also the highlight of the Feast of Aishura, which takes place on the tenth day of the month of Moharrem (the first month of the Moslem lunar calendar). On Aishura, families gather to honor the memory of their ancestors and to partake of a communal platter of couscous. Some superstitious wives use the occasion to ensure their husband's continuing fidelity by concealing tender morsels of *qaddid*, preserved lamb's tail, within the mound of couscous.

Traditionally, couscous is cooked in a *q'dra*, a pot-bellied vessel that holds the stew, capped with a *keskes*, a tight-fitting colander containing the granules. The *q'dra* was originally made of terra-cotta, and the *keskes* of woven alfalfa stalks. Both implements are still used in more remote regions of the Maghreb. For the most part, however, modern domestic *couscoussiers*, as the two implements are known collectively in French, are made of aluminum or stainless steel.

During the cooking process, the gap between the two elements of the *couscoussier* is sealed with a strip of cloth dipped in water and flour, to ensure that steam rising from the broth will pass directly through the granules in the colander above. A relatively recent innovation has made the steaming process more efficient. A standard pressure cooker, known in French as a *cocotte minute*, takes the place of the *q'dra*. The steam-exhaust valve of the pressure cooker fits securely through a hole at the apex of an unusual, funnel-shaped aluminum colander that is filled with couscous.

When Moroccans eat couscous from a communal platter, they deftly fashion little balls of the broth-soaked granules with the first three fingers of their right hand, and pop them into their mouths with a flick of the thumb, as Pierre Loti so aptly described it. Uninitiated diners may prefer to confront the dish armed with a soup spoon.

The influx of immigrants from the Maghreb and of *Pieds-Noirs* (French citizens born in North Africa) to Europe, and to France in particular, is largely responsible for the increasing international popularity of North African cuisine over the past forty years. Recent polls show that French restaurant patrons rank couscous as their third-favorite meal behind *steak-frites* and the classic leg of lamb with flageolet beans!

Thanks in large part to European connoisseurs, couscous has broken free from its traditional territorial boundaries and is rapidly becoming one of the world's most recognizable dishes. Along with other international foods such as French croissants, Italian pizza, and Chinese egg rolls, couscous is featured on menus as far flung as Singapore and Australia. Chefs the world over, discovering the exciting versatility of couscous, are developing innovative combinations, such as the one for Salsa Couscous Chicken, which won first prize in the 1997 Pillsbury Bake-Off, and the exotic kangaroo couscous I saw on the menu of an elegant restaurant in the wine country outside Adelaide, Australia.

Inspired by such creative ideas for fusion couscous, I have developed my own cosmopolitan, kitchen-tested recipes—from Vietnamese Couscous Salad (page 60) and Couscous Quenelles Florentine (page 102) to Coconut Milk Couscous Curry with Seared Scallops (page 100) and Couscous Mango Mousse (page 108). I present them to you in this book, along with a personal selection of time-honored, traditional North African favorites.

BASICS

techniques

STEAMING COUSCOUS IN THE TRADITIONAL MANNER

Throughout this book, for the sake of convenience, I have given directions only for the instant cooking method. However, you always have the option of steaming couscous in the traditional manner, the way it is done in most Moroccan kitchens. To do this, in a large pot or in the bottom element of a *couscoussier*, bring water or broth to a rolling boil. Meanwhile, in a shallow bowl, mix 1 cup couscous with ¾ cup water. Let stand until the liquid is absorbed, 5 to 10 minutes. Place the moist couscous into a colander that fits tightly over the pot, or into the top element of the *couscoussier*. Seal the seam between the two elements with a strip of cloth covered with a thin paste of flour and water. Cook, uncovered, until steam emanates from the surface of the couscous granules, 10 to 12 minutes.

Transfer the couscous to a large, shallow bowl. Add a small amount of olive oil, butter, or *smen* (see page 24) as the recipe dictates. Using your fingers, rake it while adding ¼ cup of water or broth. Let stand 5 to 10 minutes. Return the couscous to the colander or the top of the *couscoussier*, and cook again until steam rises through the couscous, 10 to 12 minutes. The couscous granules will triple in size during the steaming process (1 cup raw couscous yielding approximately 3 cups cooked).

Return the couscous to the large, shallow bowl. Rake again with your fingers to break up any lumps. The couscous granules should be light and fluffy. At this point, you can proceed as directed in the recipe.

TOASTING NUTS

Toasting nuts intensifies their flavor. To toast on top of the stove: Place nuts in a dry, nonstick skillet over medium-high heat. Shake the pan back and forth, or stir with a wooden spoon until the nuts turn a light brown, 2 to 3 minutes. To toast in the oven: Preheat the oven to 375 degrees F. Place the nuts in one layer on a nonstick baking sheet. Bake, stirring occasionally, until lightly browned, 12 to 15 minutes. Let cool.

USING SAFFRON

To release the intense flavor of saffron, toast the threads or dissolve them in liquid before combining them with the other ingredients. To toast: Place the threads in a small nonstick skillet over medium-high heat and stir constantly until they release their distinctive aroma, 50 seconds to 1 minute. Transfer to a mortar and pestle. Add a pinch of salt and grind to a fine powder. To dissolve: Put the saffron threads in 1/4 cup warm broth or water. If using the latter technique, make sure to subtract 1/4 cup of liquid from the amount called for in the recipe.

PEELING AND SEEDING TOMATOES

Make two small, intersecting cuts on the blossom end of each tomato. In a medium saucepan filled with boiling water, blanch the tomatoes for 20 to 30 seconds. Remove them with a slotted spoon, and let cool. Peel off the skins with your fingers. Cut the tomatoes in half, and gently squeeze out the seeds.

GRILLING PEPPERS

Over an open flame or under a broiler, grill the peppers, turning them carefully with tongs, until the skins blister and blacken, 8 to 10 minutes. Transfer to a bowl or plastic bag, and seal. Let cool. Peel, seed, and derib the peppers. Set over a colander to drain. Proceed with the recipe, or refrigerate for later use.

ROASTING GARLIC

Preheat the oven to 375 degrees F. Remove the papery husk from several heads of garlic, but do not separate into individual cloves. Place them in a small, ovenproof dish. Bake, uncovered, 50 minutes to 1 hour. The garlic is ready when the pulp squeezes easily from a clove. Roasted garlic will keep for 2 to 3 weeks in an airtight container in the refrigerator.

condiments

MOROCCAN PRESERVED LEMONS

Preserved lemon is one condiment Moroccan cooks simply cannot do without.

Makes 1 quart

12 unblemished lemons of equal size
Sea salt or table salt

1 • Scrub the lemons under running water and pat dry. Cut a thin slice from each end of a lemon. Set on end and make a vertical cut three quarters of the way through the fruit, leaving the two halves attached. Turn the lemon upside down, rotate 90 degrees, and make a second vertical cut, again three quarters of the way through the fruit. Fill each cut with as much salt as it will hold. Place the lemon in a sterilized, 1-quart-size, wide-mouth canning jar. Proceed in this manner for the remaining lemons, pressing as many into the jar as possible. Seal and set aside at room temperature. Add additional lemons over the next few days as the rinds of the first lemons begin to soften. By this time, the juice should have risen to cover the lemons. If not, add 1 tablespoon of fresh lemon juice mixed with 1 teaspoon of salt. This will prevent the top lemons from darkening. Store at room temperature until the rinds become tender, and the pulp acquires the consistency of jam, 3 to 4 weeks. Refrigerate. Use within 6 months.

SMEN/MOROCCAN PRESERVED BUTTER

Preserved butter, with its deep, pungent aroma and distinctive flavor, enhances many of Morocco's savory dishes, especially couscous.

Makes 1½ cups

1 pound unsalted butter (pasteurized or unpasteurized)
2 teaspoons dried oregano leaves
1 tablespoon sea salt

1 · In a medium saucepan, melt the butter over low heat. Wrap the oregano in a small piece of cheesecloth. Tie the sachet with cotton string, and set in the butter. Simmer until the butter separates into a clear, golden liquid and a milky sediment, 25 to 30 minutes. Carefully pour off the golden liquid (clarified butter), and strain through a piece of clean, fine muslin. Discard the milky sediment and oregano sachet. Transfer to a hot sterilized glass jar. Add the salt and mix until dissolved. Cover and let stand in a cool place until the mixture becomes pungent, 1 to 2 weeks. Drain any liquid from the jar and refrigerate the butter. Use within 6 months.

HARISSA/NORTH AFRICAN HOT SAUCE

The popularity of harissa, *the Tunisian condiment par excellence, has spread throughout North Africa. Tunisians mix it liberally with almost every dish, while Algerians and Moroccans prefer to serve it on the side, adding it according to individual taste. The piquancy of your* harissa *will depend upon the variety of dried chile peppers you select. For mild* harissa, *use New Mexico red or guajillo; for medium, pasilla or chipotle; and use cayenne or habanero for the hottest* harissa. *Wear protective rubber gloves when working with chiles. Do not rub your eyes!*

Makes about 1 cup

12 dried chile peppers
4 garlic cloves, minced
½ cup extra-virgin olive oil, plus extra for topping
1 teaspoon salt, or to taste
1 teaspoon ground cumin, or to taste

1 • Wearing rubber gloves, open the chiles. Remove and discard the seeds. With scissors, cut the chiles into small pieces. Place in a bowl of warm water and soak until they soften, 25 to 30 minutes.

2 • Drain the peppers and squeeze out any remaining water. Place them in a blender with the garlic, olive oil, salt, and cumin. Process until smooth. Transfer to a sterilized pint jar. Cover with a thin layer of oil. Use within 6 months.

NOTE: *You can find commercial* harissa *in cans or tubes in Middle Eastern markets and in some large supermarkets. If it is unavailable, substitute Tabasco sauce, Thai hot sauce, or Indonesian* sambal manis.

TRADITIONAL RECIPES

SICILIAN FISH CUSCUSÙ ALLA TRAPANESE

According to food historian Clifford Wright, Arab invaders from North Africa may have been the first to introduce couscous to Sicily, sometime in the twelfth or thirteenth century. Second-generation Sicilian-American Sharon Perna, a citrus grower from Southern California, carries on family tradition when she prepares this elegant dish, a specialty from her grandparents' native province of Trapani, on Sicily's western coast.

Serves 6

18 mussels (see Note)
12 littleneck clams, scrubbed
½ cup white wine
4 cups water
2½ extra-large fish-flavored bouillon cubes
   (see Note)
3 tablespoons olive oil
2 medium onions, finely diced
3 ribs celery, finely diced
2 carrots, peeled and finely diced
2 garlic cloves, minced
One 14¼-ounce can crushed tomatoes in
   tomato purée
2 bay leaves
10 sprigs fresh flat-leaf parsley,
   tied with cotton string
1 teaspoon sweet Hungarian paprika
8 threads Spanish saffron (see page 22)
1½ cups couscous
Two 1-inch-thick swordfish fillets
Four 1-inch-thick sea bass or halibut fillets
8 ounces medium shrimp, shelled and deveined
½ teaspoon hot red pepper flakes for garnish

1 • In a medium nonreactive casserole or a heavy skillet over high heat, place the mussels and clams, and add the wine. Cover and cook until the shellfish open, 8 to 10 minutes. With a slotted spoon, transfer them to a bowl and set aside. Discard any unopened shellfish. Strain the cooking liquid (about 1 cup) through a fine meshed sieve lined with a paper towel. In a medium saucepan, bring the strained liquid, the water, and the fish bouillon cubes to a boil. Stir until the bouillon cubes dissolve, 2 to 3 minutes. Transfer to a bowl and set aside.

2 • In the same pan over medium-high heat, warm 2 tablespoons of the olive oil. Cook the onions, stirring occasionally until golden, 4 to 5 minutes. Add the celery, carrots, and garlic. Cook, stirring to blend, 2 or 3 minutes. Add the tomatoes, bay leaves, parsley, paprika, and saffron. Cook, stirring to blend, 1 to 2 minutes. Add 3 cups of the reserved broth. Reduce heat to medium. Cook, covered, until the sauce thickens somewhat, 20 to 25 minutes. Discard the parsley and bay leaves. Set aside.

(continued)

3 • Preheat the oven to 200 degrees F. While the tomato sauce is cooking, in a medium saucepan over medium-high heat, bring the remaining 2 cups of broth and remaining olive oil to a boil. Add the couscous in a stream. Stir once. Remove from the heat. Cover and keep warm in the oven.

4 • Ten minutes before serving, bring the tomato sauce to a low boil. Add the swordfish. Three minutes later, add the sea bass, shrimp, and shellfish. Heat through, 2 to 3 minutes. Remove from the heat.

5 • Fluff the couscous with a fork and mound the couscous in the center of a warm serving platter. Pour 1 cup of the tomato sauce over the couscous. Top with the seafood and the shellfish. Pour the remaining sauce over the dish. Sprinkle with hot pepper flakes. Serve immediately.

NOTE: *Do not purchase mussels or clams with open shells. To clean mussels, scrub them under running water. Remove the soft, tufted, exterior growth, called a "byssal thread," by which they attach themselves to rocks.*

Fish bouillon cubes are available in Asian and Mexican markets and in specialty food stores.

ROCK CORNISH GAME HENS WITH DRIED FRUIT AND COUSCOUS STUFFING

Casablancans call this exotic stuffing zamita. *They use it with pigeon, chicken, turkey, and sometimes, whole fish.*

Serves 2 to 4

2½ **cups chicken broth**
4 **tablespoons butter**
10 **threads Spanish saffron** (see page 22)
½ **cup couscous**
2 **tablespoons olive oil**
1 **teaspoon ground turmeric**
½ **teaspoon sweet Hungarian paprika**
Two 12-ounce **Cornish game hens**
½ **cup** (about 4 ounces) **slivered blanched almonds, toasted** (see page 20)
1 **cup** (about 5 ounces) **golden raisins**
½ **cup** (about 5 ounces) **pitted prunes, coarsely chopped**
2 **tablespoons honey**
¾ **teaspoon ground cinnamon**
½ **teaspoon ground ginger**
½ **teaspoon salt**
¼ **teaspoon freshly ground pepper**
1 **medium onion, diced**

1 • Preheat the oven to 425 degrees F. In a medium saucepan, bring ¾ cup of the broth, 2 tablespoons of butter, and half of the saffron to a boil. Add the couscous in a stream. Stir once. Remove from the heat. Cover and let stand until couscous is tender, 12 to 15 minutes. Set aside.

2 • In a large bowl, mix the olive oil with the remaining saffron, the turmeric, and paprika.

Using your hands, coat the hens inside and out with this mixture. Set aside.

3 • In a medium bowl, combine 1 tablespoon of the slivered almonds with the raisins, prunes, 1 tablespoon of the honey, ½ teaspoon of the cinnamon, ¼ teaspoon of the ginger, ¼ teaspoon of the salt, ⅛ teaspoon of the pepper, and the remaining butter. Set aside.

4 • In a food processor, in increments, grind the dried fruit and spice mixture until it acquires a thick, gritty consistency. Transfer to a medium bowl and combine with the couscous.

5 • With a large spoon, stuff equal portions of the couscous mixture into each hen. Place them, breast side down, in a medium baking dish. They should not touch. Surround them with diced onion and add the remaining broth. Cover and bake 50 to 55 minutes. Turn hens over and baste. Bake, breast side up, uncovered, until the hens are brown and the juices run clear when a thigh is pierced with a fork, 30 to 35 minutes. Transfer hens to a warm serving platter. Keep warm.

6 • Drain the pan juices into a medium saucepan over medium heat. Add the remaining honey, cinnamon, ginger, salt, and pepper. Reduce by a quarter. Spoon over and around the hens. Sprinkle with remaining almonds and serve.

FENNEL COUSCOUS TUNISIENNE

Tunisians use a unique seasoning called tabil, *a blend of coriander, caraway, peppercorns, dried garlic, and dried chile peppers, to flavor this dish. Harissa, a fiery North African condiment, would certainly not be an optional ingredient in Tunisia, a country where the people like their food hot!*

Serves 6

6 medium fennel bulbs, with fronds
4 large leeks
4 tablespoons olive oil
1½ pounds boneless beef chuck roast
3 tablespoons tomato paste
6 cups water
2 mild green chiles
2 tablespoons *tabil* (see Note)
6 chicken thighs
4 medium carrots, peeled and cut into sticks
4 teaspoons salt
½ teaspoon freshly ground pepper
1⅓ cups broth
1 cup couscous
Harissa hot sauce (optional, page 25)
     for serving

1 • Trim and reserve the tough stalks from the fennel bulbs. Remove the feathery fronds from the stalks. Finely chop the fronds. Set aside.

2 • Quarter the bulbs and rinse them under running water. Set aside.

3 • Rinse the leeks thoroughly under running water to remove the grit. Cut the green tops from the leeks and tie them with cotton string. Set the white stalks aside.

4 • In a large soup pot over medium-high heat, heat 2 tablespoons of the olive oil. Cook the beef, turning occasionally, until lightly browned, 3 to 4 minutes. Add the tomato paste, and stir to coat. Add the water, fennel stalks, green leek tops, chiles, and *tabil* spice blend. Reduce heat to medium. Cover and cook until the meat is tender, 1½ to 2 hours. Preheat the oven to 200 degrees F. Discard the leek tops and fennel stalks. With a slotted spoon, transfer the meat to an ovenproof dish and keep warm in the oven.

5 • To the sauce add the chicken thighs, carrots, remaining white stalks of the leeks, the fennel bulbs, 1 tablespoon of the salt, and the pepper. Cover and cook until the chicken and the fennel bulbs are tender, 35 to 40 minutes. With a slotted spoon, transfer the chicken, carrots, and leeks to the ovenproof dish. Keep the sauce simmering on the stove.

6 • In a large skillet over medium-high heat, heat 1 tablespoon of the olive oil. With a slotted spoon, transfer the fennel bulbs to the skillet. Cook, turning occasionally, until browned, 6 to 8 minutes.

7 • Meanwhile, in a small saucepan, bring the broth and the remaining salt and olive oil to a boil. Remove from the heat. Add the couscous and the reserved chopped fennel fronds. Stir once. Cover and let stand until the couscous is tender, 12 to 15 minutes. Fluff with a fork.

8 • Heap the couscous in the center of large, warm serving platter. Arrange the fennel bulbs, carrots, and leeks over the couscous. Distribute the chiles, meat, and chicken thighs around the base of the couscous. Moisten the dish with 1 cup of the sauce. Serve with the remaining sauce and *harissa*, if using, on the side.

N O T E : *To make your own* tabil, *combine 3 tablespoons ground coriander, 1 tablespoon ground caraway, 1 tablespoon garlic powder, and 1 tablespoon mild Mexican ground chile powder. Store in an airtight container. Use within 2 months. Makes about ⅓ cup.*

ALGERIAN COUSCOUS WITH LAMB MEATBALLS, LIMA BEANS, AND ARTICHOKE HEARTS

In Algerian Sephardic Jewish homes, meatballs often accompany a steaming platter of couscous. The meatballs are precooked, then reheated in the broth just a few minutes before serving.

Serves 8

STEW
2 tablespoons olive oil
2 large onions, coarsely chopped
2½ pounds lamb shoulder
3 garlic cloves, peeled
25 sprigs fresh cilantro, tied with cotton string
30 sprigs fresh flat-leaf parsley,
    tied with cotton string
3 rutabagas, quartered
6 cups chicken or beef broth
3 ribs celery
4 zucchini, quartered
One 10-ounce package frozen lima beans
One 14¼-ounce can artichoke hearts,
    drained and rinsed
1½ teaspoons salt
½ teaspoon freshly ground pepper

MEATBALLS
1 pound ground lamb
20 sprigs fresh flat-leaf parsley, chopped
15 sprigs fresh cilantro leaves, chopped
4 garlic cloves, minced
1 egg, lightly beaten
5 tablespoons unseasoned bread crumbs
¼ teaspoon ground cinnamon
1 teaspoon salt
¼ teaspoon freshly ground pepper
1 tablespoon water
1 tablespoon olive oil

COUSCOUS
2⅔ cups chicken broth
1 tablespoon olive oil
2 teaspoons salt
2 cups couscous

Harissa hot sauce for serving (optional, page 25)

1 • To make the stew: In the bottom part of a *couscoussier* or a large soup pot over medium-high heat, warm 2 tablespoons of the olive oil. Cook the onions until wilted, 4 to 5 minutes. Add the lamb and cook, stirring occasionally, until browned, 5 to 6 minutes. Add the garlic, cilantro, parsley, rutabagas, and broth. Bring to a boil and then simmer until the lamb is tender, 1½ to 2 hours.

2 • Preheat the oven to 200 degrees F. With a slotted spoon, transfer the rutabagas to an ovenproof dish. Cover and keep warm in the oven. Let the lamb cool. Remove and discard the bones. Add the meat to the vegetables in the oven.

3 • To the broth, add the celery, zucchini, lima beans, and artichoke hearts. Cover and cook over low heat until the zucchini are tender, 15 to 20 minutes. Using a slotted spoon, remove the vegetables and add to those in the oven. Discard the cilantro and parsley. Season the broth with the salt and pepper and keep it simmering on the stove.

(continued)

4 • **To make the meatballs:** In a large bowl combine the ground lamb, parsley, cilantro, garlic, egg, bread crumbs, cinnamon, salt, pepper, and water. Blend thoroughly with your hands. Shape the ground meat mixture into meatballs 1 inch in diameter. Set aside.

5 • In a large skillet over medium-high heat, heat the olive oil. Add the meatballs, and cook until they are browned on all sides, 8 to 10 minutes. With a slotted spoon, transfer to an ovenproof dish and keep warm.

6 • **To make the couscous:** In a medium saucepan, bring the 2⅔ cups broth, the olive oil, and salt to a boil. Add the couscous in a stream. Stir once. Remove from the heat. Cover and let stand until the couscous is tender, 12 to 15 minutes. Fluff with a fork.

7 • Ten minutes before serving, add the meatballs to the simmering broth, and heat through. Mound the couscous on a large, warm serving platter. Top with the cooked vegetables, the lamb, and the meatballs. Pour 1 cup of the broth over the dish to moisten. Serve with remaining broth and *harissa*, if using, on the side.

SPICY TUNISIAN COUSCOUS SOUP

My friends Jim and Froukje Frost spent several years in Tunisia, one of the North African countries where couscous is a staple. Froukje often makes this soup from leftover couscous. Tunisians flavor almost every dish with fiery harissa *(hot sauce). Use it as liberally as you dare!*

Serves 6

2 tablespoons olive oil
1 medium onion, coarsely chopped
3 tablespoons tomato paste
2 teaspoons ground coriander
2 teaspoons ground cumin
5 garlic cloves, minced
1 teaspoon *Harissa* hot sauce (optional, page 25), plus extra for serving
6 chicken legs or thighs
3 small tomatoes, peeled, seeded (see page 22), and coarsely chopped
1 large carrot, peeled, and cut into ¼-inch slices
1 medium potato, peeled and cubed
6 ounces pumpkin or winter squash, peeled and cut into ½-inch cubes
8 cups chicken broth
1 medium zucchini, cut into ¼-inch slices
One 14¼-ounce can garbanzo beans, drained
⅓ cup couscous
Salt and freshly ground pepper to taste

1 • In a large soup pot or Dutch oven, heat the oil over medium-high heat. Cook the onion, stirring occasionally until golden, 4 to 5 minutes. Add the tomato paste, coriander, cumin, garlic, and *harissa*, if using. Stir to blend. Add the chicken. Stir to coat. Reduce heat to medium. Add the tomatoes, carrot, potato, pumpkin, and broth. Cover and cook until the vegetables are tender, 35 to 40 minutes.

2 • With a slotted spoon, transfer 2 cups of the vegetables to a bowl, and ladle in 2 cups of the broth. Let cool. Transfer to a blender or food processor, and purée until smooth. Return to the pot.

3 • With a slotted spoon, transfer the chicken to a plate. When cool enough to handle, remove the skin and bones. Return the boned chicken to the pot.

4 • Add the zucchini, garbanzo beans, and couscous. Continue cooking until the couscous is tender, 12 to 15 minutes. Season with salt and pepper. Serve with extra *harissa* on the side, if using.

BERBER BARLEY GRIT COUSCOUS
WITH WINTER VEGETABLES

Couscous belboula, *made from barley grits, is a specialty of Morocco's indigenous Berbers, many of whom live in the barley-producing region of the country. This dish was the pièce de résistance of a memorable dinner I had in the village of Sidi Abdesalem, in the heart of the Middle Atlas Mountains. Local cooks often moisten couscous with equal parts of broth and milk. Be sure to preheat the serving platter in order to keep the dish warm during the lengthy process of assembly.*

Serves 6

2 tablespoons vegetable oil

2½ pounds lamb shoulder, cut into 2-inch chunks

2 medium onions, thinly sliced

8 cups beef broth

30 sprigs fresh cilantro, tied with cotton string

15 sprigs fresh flat-leaf parsley,
    tied with cotton string

12 threads Spanish saffron (see page 22)

2 teaspoons ground turmeric

2 teaspoons ground ginger

1 teaspoon ground cinnamon

1 teaspoon sweet Hungarian paprika

4 medium rutabagas, quartered

2 pounds winter squash, peeled
    and cut into 2-inch pieces

6 medium carrots, cut crosswise into 3-inch pieces,
    and lengthwise into sticks

4 teaspoons salt

½ teaspoon freshly ground pepper

1½ cups instant barley grits (see Note)

1 tablespoon butter

1 tablespoon *Smen* (optional, page 24)

1 cup half-and-half, heated

1 • In the bottom part of a *couscoussier* or a stockpot, heat the oil over medium-high heat. Add the lamb and cook, turning with tongs until browned on all sides, 5 to 6 minutes. Add the onions. Cook, stirring occasionally until they soften, 4 to 5 minutes. Add 6 cups of the broth, the cilantro, and parsley. Bring to a rolling boil. With a slotted spoon, skim off the foam. Reduce heat to low. Add the saffron, turmeric, ginger, cinnamon, paprika, and rutabagas. Simmer, covered, until the rutabagas are tender, 55 minutes to 1 hour. Preheat the oven to 200 degrees F. With a slotted spoon, transfer the rutabagas to a baking dish. Cover and keep warm in the oven.

2 • To the broth, add the winter squash and the carrots. Cook, covered, until the vegetables are tender, 25 to 30 minutes. With a slotted spoon, transfer them to the baking dish in the oven. Discard the cilantro and parsley. Season the broth with the salt and pepper. Keep simmering until ready to serve.

3 • Meanwhile, prepare the barley grits. In a large saucepan over medium-high heat, bring the remaining beef broth and the butter to a boil. Add the barley grits in a stream. Stir once. Remove from the heat. Add the *smen*, if using. Cover and let stand until the grits are tender, 12 to 15 minutes.

4 • In a heat-proof bowl, combine the warm half-and half with 2 cups of the hot broth. Mound the grits in the center of a large, warm serving platter. Moisten with some of the broth and half-and-half mixture. Place several chunks of meat on the mound of barley grits, and the rest, along with the vegetables, around the base. Serve with the remaining broth mixture on the side.

NOTE: *Boxes of instant barley grits are available in the cereal section of health food stores.*

MOROCCAN SWEET COUSCOUS WITH ALMONDS, RAISINS, AND ORANGE BLOSSOM WATER

Sweet couscous, called s'ffa, *is made from the finest grade of couscous. It is prepared on special occasions such as weddings, births, or religious celebrations. In Morocco, s'ffa is usually served with a glass of* l'ben, *a soured milk product similar to American buttermilk. I prefer to drizzle a little buttermilk over the warm couscous at serving time.*

Makes 3 cups

4 tablespoons butter
1 cup whole blanched almonds
1⅓ cups water
½ teaspoon salt
½ cup (about 3 ounces) golden raisins
1 cup couscous
2 tablespoons orange blossom water (see Note)
3 tablespoons granulated sugar
¼ cup ground cinnamon
¼ cup confectioners' sugar
Buttermilk for serving

1 • In a medium skillet, heat 2 tablespoons of the butter over medium-high heat. Fry the almonds, stirring occasionally, until they are golden brown, 5 to 6 minutes. Set aside.

2 • In a medium saucepan over medium heat, bring the water, salt, raisins, and remaining butter to a boil. Add the couscous in a stream. Stir once. Remove from the heat. Cover and let stand until the couscous is tender, 12 to 15 minutes. Transfer the couscous to a bowl. Blend with the orange blossom water and granulated sugar.

3 • Heap the couscous into the center of a warm serving platter. Using your hands, fashion into a conical shape. Garnish with almonds, cinnamon, and confectioners' sugar. Serve warm, with buttermilk on the side. Place several saucers of sugar and cinnamon around the table, so that they can be added to taste.

NOTE: *Orange blossom water is available in Middle Eastern markets and in some liquor stores.*

BEEF COUSCOUS WITH PRUNES, BUTTERNUT SQUASH, AND CARAMELIZED ONIONS

*The blending of sweet and savory is one of the characteristics of Moroccan cuisine.
I frequently serve the butternut squash and caramelized onion mixture on its own, as a
side dish to accompany roast chicken or turkey.*

Serves 6

1½ pounds butternut squash
3 large onions
4 tablespoons olive oil
1 teaspoon ground turmeric
1 teaspoon ground ginger
1¼ teaspoons ground mace
1 teaspoon freshly ground pepper
2 pounds boneless beef chuck roast,
   trimmed and cut into 1½-inch cubes
½ teaspoon freshly ground pepper
2 garlic cloves, minced
3⅓ cups beef broth
1 cup (about 12 ounces) pitted prunes
2½ teaspoons salt
1 tablespoon honey
½ cup (about 3 ounces) seedless raisins,
   plumped in warm water and drained
1 cup couscous
¼ cup sliced almonds, toasted (see page 20)

1• Preheat the oven to 350 degrees F. Place the squash in an ovenproof dish. Bake until fairly tender, 30 to 35 minutes. Remove from the oven. When cool enough to handle, peel the squash. Cut into circular sections about ½ inch thick. Cut each section in half. Set aside.

2• Finely slice 2 of the onions. Set aside.

3• Dice the remaining onion. In a medium Dutch oven or nonreactive casserole dish, heat 2 tablespoons of the olive oil over medium-high heat. Add the diced onion, turmeric, ginger, mace, and half of the pepper. Cook, stirring, until the spices coat the onion, 1 to 2 minutes. Add the beef and the garlic. Cook, stirring, until the beef is lightly browned, 3 to 4 minutes. Add 2 cups of the broth. Cover, first with foil, then with a lid, and place in the oven. Bake until the beef is partially cooked, 50 to 55 minutes. Remove from the oven. Add the prunes and the partially baked squash. Replace the foil and lid, and bake until the meat is tender, 40 to 45 minutes. Season with 1 teaspoon of the salt. Set aside.

4 • Meanwhile, in a medium skillet over medium heat, warm 1 tablespoon of the olive oil. Cook the sliced onions with the honey until the onions turn the color of light caramel, 40 to 45 minutes. Add the raisins, and cook 10 to 15 minutes longer. Season with ½ teaspoon of the salt and the remaining pepper. Set aside.

5 • In a medium saucepan, bring the remaining 1⅓ cups broth, 1 teaspoon salt, and 1 tablespoon olive oil to a boil. Add the couscous in a stream. Stir once. Remove from the heat. Cover and let stand until the couscous is tender, 12 to 15 minutes. Fluff the couscous with a fork.

6 • Mound the couscous on a warm serving platter. Push the bottom of a wide bowl into the center of the couscous to form a shallow depression. Fill with the meat and top with the onion-raisin mixture, and moisten with some of the sauce. Set the squash in a scalloped pattern around the base of the couscous. Garnish with the almonds. Serve with the remaining sauce on the side.

CONTEMPORARY RECIPES

APPETIZERS
SOUPS
SALADS

STUFFED SQUASH BLOSSOMS WITH GOAT CHEESE—PESTO COUSCOUS

Look for fresh squash blossoms at your local farmer's market or specialty produce market. In California, I am able to find them almost year round. Serve these stuffed blossoms as a first course or as the main dish for a light summer luncheon.

Makes 18 blossoms

2 tablespoons olive oil

1 medium onion, finely diced

3 garlic cloves, minced

12 plum tomatoes (about 2 pounds), peeled, seeded (see page 22), and coarsely chopped

1 bay leaf

1 tablespoon herbes de Provence

Salt and freshly ground pepper to taste

1½ cups chicken broth

¾ cup couscous

1 egg, lightly beaten

1 tablespoon basil pesto

3 ounces crumbled goat cheese

18 squash blossoms (see Note)

1 • In a medium skillet or pan that can go from stove to table, heat 1 tablespoon of the olive oil over medium heat. Cook the onion and the garlic, stirring occasionally, until the onion turns golden, 4 to 5 minutes. Add the tomatoes, bay leaf, and herbes de Provence. Cook, stirring occasionally, until the sauce thickens somewhat, 15 to 20 minutes. Discard the bay leaf. Season with salt and pepper. Set aside.

2 • Meanwhile, in a medium saucepan over medium-high heat, bring 1 cup of the broth and remaining olive oil to a boil. Remove from the heat. Add the couscous in a stream. Stir once. Cover and set aside until couscous is tender, 12 to 15 minutes. Stir in the egg, pesto, and cheese.

3 • Fill each blossom with 2 to 3 heaping teaspoons of the couscous mixture. Gently twist each blossom closed, and set in the skillet with the tomato sauce. Proceed in this manner with all the blossoms. Pour the remaining ½ cup of broth around the blossoms. Return to low heat. Cover and simmer until they are cooked through, 10 to 12 minutes. Serve immediately.

NOTE : *Select large, open blossoms. Handle them gently. If the blossom is still attached to a baby squash, carefully cut the stem between the flower and squash. Reserve the squash for another use. Carefully spread the petals to remove the stamen and pistils. Rinse the inside of each blossom with cold water, and set upside down in a colander to drain until you're ready to fill it.*

MUSHROOMS WITH COUSCOUS, FETA CHEESE, PINE NUTS, AND SUN-DRIED TOMATOES

A quartet of Mediterranean ingredients elevate prosaic stuffed mushrooms into an elegant hors d'oeuvre. For this recipe I use dry-packed sun-dried tomatoes. You can substitute sun-dried tomatoes packed in oil. If doing so, omit the olive oil called for in the recipe. Also eliminate the soaking process.

Makes 1 dozen mushroom caps

3 tablespoons finely diced sun-dried tomatoes
¾ cup chicken broth
¼ cup couscous
12 large mushrooms (about 2 inches in diameter), wiped clean, and stems removed and reserved
1 tablespoon olive oil
2 tablespoons pine nuts, toasted (see page 20)
2 green onions, green tops included, finely diced
4 ounces feta cheese, crumbled
1 egg yolk, lightly beaten with 1 teaspoon water
⅛ teaspoon freshly ground pepper
Chopped parsley for garnish

1 • In a small bowl filled with warm water, soak the sun-dried tomatoes until soft, about 10 minutes. Drain. Set aside.

2 • Meanwhile, in a medium saucepan, bring the broth to a boil. Add the couscous in a stream. Stir once. Remove from the heat. Cover and let stand until couscous is tender, 12 to 15 minutes. Set aside. Finely mince the mushroom stems. Set aside.

3 • In a medium skillet over medium-high heat, warm the olive oil. Cook the pine nuts, stirring occasionally, until golden, 3 to 4 minutes. Add the onions, minced stems, and sun-dried tomatoes. Cook until the stems are tender, 3 to 4 minutes. With a slotted spoon, transfer the mixture to a medium bowl. Set aside.

4 • To the same skillet, add the mushroom caps and 2 tablespoons water. Cover and cook, turning them over once, until the caps are browned, 2 minutes on each side. Place them snugly in a 9-by-13-inch baking dish. Set aside.

5 • Preheat the oven to 425 degrees F. In a medium bowl, combine the couscous, onion-mushroom mixture, feta cheese, egg yolk, and pepper. Spoon 1 heaping tablespoon of the mixture into each cap. Pour ½ cup water around the mushrooms. Cover the dish tightly with foil. Bake until the caps are tender, 15 to 20 minutes. Garnish with chopped parsley, and serve.

GRAPE LEAVES FILLED WITH COUSCOUS AND GROUND LAMB

Use either fresh or preserved grape leaves to prepare these unconventional Greek dolmas. In either case, the leaves should be blanched in boiling water.

Makes about thirty 2½-inch grape leaves

One 8-ounce jar grape leaves, drained
12 ounces ground lamb
1 medium onion, finely diced
4 garlic cloves, minced
1 medium carrot, peeled and finely diced
2 tablespoons pine nuts
2 teaspoons ground cinnamon
½ cup couscous
4 tablespoons chopped fresh mint leaves
2 eggs, lightly beaten
4 tablespoons fresh lemon juice
1½ teaspoons salt
¼ teaspoon freshly ground pepper
3 tablespoons olive oil
2 cups beef broth
Lemon wedges for serving

YOGURT SAUCE
1 cup plain yogurt
2 tablespoons chopped fresh mint leaves
½ cucumber, peeled, seeded, and finely diced

1 • In a large saucepan filled with boiling water, blanch the grape leaves, 3 or 4 at a time, for 10 to 15 seconds. Transfer the leaves to a baking sheet lined with paper towels to drain. Set aside. When the leaves are cool enough to handle, remove the stems with kitchen scissors or a sharp knife. Set aside.

2 • In a large bowl, combine the lamb, onion, garlic, carrot, pine nuts, cinnamon, couscous, mint, eggs, 1 tablespoon of the lemon juice, the salt, and pepper. Mix well with your hands. Set aside.

3 • To assemble, set a leaf on a flat surface, shiny side down, stem end towards you. With your hands, form 1 tablespoon of filling into a sausage shape about 2 inches long. Center it horizontally in the widest part of the leaf. Fold up the bottom of the leaf to partially cover the filling. Fold over the sides. Roll up into a plump "cigar" about 2½ inches long (see Note). Continue in this manner until all the filling has been used. Set the stuffed leaves snugly in a Dutch oven or heavy pan. Arrange a second layer of dolmas at 90 degrees to the first.

4 • Drizzle the olive oil over the leaves. Add the remaining lemon juice and enough broth to barely cover the leaves. Weight the dolmas with a small, ovenproof bowl filled with water and set on top of a heat-proof plate. Cover the pan. Cook over medium heat until the leaves are tender, 35 to 40 minutes. Set aside to cool in pan juices.

5 • Prepare the sauce by combining the yogurt, mint, and cucumber. Transfer the dolmas to a platter. Serve with lemon wedges.

NOTE: *If the leaves are quite large, trim their tops and sides, to avoid having too much leaf in the finished roll.*

CHICKEN VEGETABLE SOUP
WITH MINT COUSCOUS DUMPLINGS

Here is a North African's answer to matzo ball soup. Unlike the traditional Jewish specialty, however, the couscous dumplings in this recipe are steamed rather than boiled.

Serves 6

2 large leeks
4 stalks celery
2 carrots
10 ¾ cups water
2 cups chopped cabbage leaves
4 pounds chicken backs, rinsed and patted dry
2 bay leaves
4 teaspoons salt
1 teaspoon finely minced lemon zest
¾ cup couscous
10 garlic cloves, roasted (see page 22)
30 fresh mint leaves, chopped (about 2 tablespoons)
¼ teaspoon freshly ground pepper
2 tablespoons butter, softened
2 eggs, lightly beaten
Lemon wedges for serving

1 • Clean the leeks under running water, being careful to remove all grit from between the leaves. Cut off the dark green leaves and reserve. Finely slice the white stalks. Set aside.

2 • Cut off the leafy fronds of the celery stalks and reserve. Finely dice the stalks. Set aside.

3 • Rinse the carrots under running water. Peel the carrots, and cut into ¼-inch slices. Set aside.

4 • In a medium saucepan over medium-high heat, combine 2 cups of the water, the leek slices, and the cabbage. Cover and cook until the vegetables are tender, 10 to 15 minutes. Let cool. Transfer to a blender or food processor, and purée until smooth. Set aside.

5 • Meanwhile, in a large soup pot, combine the chicken backs and 8 cups of the water. Bring to a boil, uncovered. After 10 minutes, with a large spoon, skim off the foam. Add the reserved leek leaves, celery fronds, the bay leaves, and puréed vegetables. Reduce heat to low. Cover and cook 1½ to 2 hours.

6 • Remove the pot from the heat. Allow the broth to cool somewhat. Strain into a large bowl. Discard the chicken backs, leek leaves, celery tops, and bay leaves. Add 2 teaspoons of the salt. Add the

(continued)

diced celery and sliced carrots. Return the broth to the pot over medium low heat. Continue cooking, covered, for another $1\frac{1}{2}$ to 2 hours. Remove from the heat. Skim off the fat (or refrigerate the soup and remove the fat after it has congealed).

7 • Meanwhile, in a medium saucepan, combine remaining $\frac{3}{4}$ cup water and the lemon zest. Bring to a boil. Add the couscous in a stream. Stir once. Remove from the heat. Cover and let stand until the couscous is tender, 12 to 15 minutes. Peel and mash the roasted garlic, and add it to the couscous, along with the mint, remaining 2 teaspoons of salt, the pepper, butter, and eggs. With your hands, blend thoroughly. Pat the couscous into a $\frac{1}{4}$-inch layer on the bottom and sides of a medium metal bowl. Refrigerate until the mixture turns puttylike, about 1 hour. From each rounded tablespoon of the couscous mixture, fashion dumplings 1 inch in diameter.

8 • Set the dumplings in a lightly oiled steamer, the top part of a *couscoussier*, or a colander, set above a pot of boiling water. Cook, covered, until the dumplings are firm, 15 to 20 minutes. In the meantime, bring the chicken soup to a simmer. With a slotted spoon, transfer the dumplings directly into the simmering soup. Cook the dumplings for 4 or 5 minutes.

9 • Ladle some soup and 3 or 4 dumplings into warm, individual soup plates. Serve immediately with lemon wedges on the side.

PERUVIAN SPINACH, COUSCOUS, AND FETA CHEESE SOUP

Cheese made from goat's milk is a traditional food of the Peruvian Andes. In this recipe, I substitute Greek feta for Peruvian goat cheese because it is more readily available. It adds a tangy flavor and silky texture to this nourishing soup.

Serves 6

8 ounces spinach, cleaned under
   running water and drained
6 cups chicken broth
36 sprigs fresh cilantro
2 tablespoons olive oil
1 medium onion, diced
2 medium potatoes, peeled and diced
2 cloves garlic, minced
1 teaspoon ground cumin
One 10-ounce package frozen baby lima beans, thawed
⅓ cup couscous
6 ounces feta or dry farmer's cheese,
   cut into ¼-inch cubes
½ teaspoon freshly ground pepper
Lemon wedges for serving

1 • Cut half of the spinach leaves into thin ribbons, reserving the stems. Set aside.

2 • In a blender, combine the reserved stems with the remaining (untrimmed) spinach, 1 cup of the broth, and the cilantro. Blend until smooth. Set aside.

3 • In a large soup pot, heat the olive oil over medium-high heat. Cook the onion, stirring occasionally, until golden, 4 to 5 minutes. Add the potatoes, garlic, and cumin. Cook, stirring, until the potatoes are well coated, 1 to 2 minutes. Add the remaining broth. Reduce heat to medium. Cover and cook until the potatoes are tender, 15 to 20 minutes. Add the ribboned spinach, the spinach-cilantro purée, lima beans, couscous, and cheese. Cook until the couscous is tender, 12 to 15 minutes. Season with the pepper. Serve with lemon wedges on the side.

COUSCOUS ONION SOUP
WITH GRUYÈRE CHEESE

Sweet onions (Vidalia, Visalia, Maui, Texas 1014, or Sweet Imperial) impart a mild and delicate flavor to this delicious soup.

Serves 6

4 tablespoons olive oil

4 large sweet onions (about 3 pounds),
   coarsely diced

4 garlic cloves, minced

2 teaspoons sugar

2 tablespoons flour

1⅓ cups red wine

4⅔ cups beef broth

½ teaspoon salt

½ cup couscous

1 cup (about 4 ounces) shredded Gruyère cheese

Chopped parsley for garnish

1 • In a large nonreactive saucepan over medium-low heat, warm 3 tablespoons of the olive oil. Cook the onions, garlic, and sugar, stirring occasionally until the onions turn a light brown, 30 to 35 minutes. Add the flour and stir to blend. Add the wine. Cook, stirring, until the mixture thickens somewhat, 4 to 5 minutes. Reduce heat to low. Add 4 cups of the broth. Cover and cook until heated through, 10 to 15 minutes.

2 • Meanwhile, in a large saucepan over medium-high heat, bring the remaining ⅔ cup broth, the salt, and remaining tablespoon of olive oil to a boil. Add the couscous in a stream. Stir once. Remove from the heat. Cover and let stand until the couscous is tender, 12 to 15 minutes.

3 • Gently pack equal amounts of couscous into 6 generously greased 6-ounce ramekins. Ladle equal servings of soup into 6 warm, shallow soup plates. Carefully unmold a ramekin of couscous into the center of each plate. Garnish with shredded cheese and parsley, and serve.

RED AND BLACK BEAN CHILI CON COUSCOUS

To chili aficionados who object to the inclusion of beans in what was originally a beef, onion, and chile pepper stew—my apologies, but I like mine with couscous!

Serves 6

3 tablespoons olive oil

2 medium onions, finely diced

½ green bell pepper, seeded and finely diced

Two 14½-ounce cans diced tomatoes

¾ cup dry red wine

2 garlic cloves, minced

1½ cups plus 2 tablespoons beef broth

40 sprigs fresh cilantro

One 28-ounce can red kidney beans

One 14½-ounce can black beans

1½ tablespoons ground cumin

1½ tablespoons mild chili powder

1 ear of corn, shucked (about ¾ cup kernels)

1½ teaspoons salt

¼ teaspoon freshly ground pepper

½ cup couscous

24 pitted green olives, finely diced

1 cup (about 4 ounces) shredded Cheddar cheese
   for serving

1 cup sour cream for serving

1 • In a large soup pot over medium-high heat, warm 2 tablespoons of the olive oil. Add the onions. Cook, stirring, until golden, 4 to 5 minutes. Add the diced pepper, and cook, stirring, until soft, 2 to 3 minutes. Add the tomatoes, wine, garlic, 1 cup of the beef broth, and half of the cilantro, tied with cotton string. Chop the remaining cilantro and set aside. Cover and cook until the soup comes to a low boil, 10 to 12 minutes. Reduce heat to medium. Add the red and black beans, cumin, chili powder, corn, 1 teaspoon of the salt, and the pepper. Cover, and continue cooking until the flavors blend, 15 to 25 minutes. Discard the cilantro.

2 • Meanwhile, in a large saucepan over medium-high heat, bring remaining broth, salt, and olive oil to a boil. Add the couscous in a stream. Stir once. Remove from the heat. Cover and let stand until the couscous is tender, 12 to 15 minutes. Stir in the chopped olives. Set aside.

3 • Gently pack equal amounts of couscous into 6 generously greased 6-ounce ramekins. Ladle equal servings of chili into 6 warm, shallow soup plates. Carefully unmold a ramekin of couscous into the center of each plate. Garnish with the shredded cheese, sour cream, and reserved chopped cilantro.

GOAT CHEESE COUSCOUS CROQUETTES EN SALADE

The crunchy couscous crust of each golden croquette surrounds a warm, soft core of chèvre *cheese. Set the croquettes in a nest of* mesclun *or mixed lettuce for an exciting first course.*

Serves 4 (makes 12 to 14 croquettes)

8 ounces soft goat cheese

1 cup couscous

¼ cup plus 2 tablespoons extra-virgin olive oil

2 tablespoons teriyaki sauce

2 tablespoons water

2 tablespoons seasoned rice vinegar

1½ teaspoons sugar

2 eggs, well beaten

Vegetable oil for frying

8 ounces *mesclun* salad mix

1 • With your hands, fashion the goat cheese into small balls about 1 inch in diameter. Coat each ball with dry couscous, then roll between the palms of your hands to embed the granules into the surface of the cheese. Refrigerate for 1 hour.

2 • In the meantime, in a large bowl, mix the olive oil, teriyaki sauce, water, rice vinegar, and sugar. Whisk until blended. Set aside.

3 • Dip each chilled cheese ball into the beaten egg. Coat again with dry couscous. In a medium skillet over medium-high heat, pour vegetable oil to a depth of 2 inches. Heat until a pinch of couscous sizzles instantly. Fry the croquettes until evenly golden, 2 to 3 minutes. With a slotted spoon, transfer them to a plate lined with paper towels to drain.

4 • Toss the *mesclun* with the dressing. Divide among 4 salad plates. Arrange 3 or 4 croquettes on each salad. Serve immediately.

COUSCOUS-PROSCIUTTO TOMATO BASKETS

Add a decorative touch to a buffet or picnic table with these attractive tomato baskets.

Serves 4 to 6

4 large or 6 medium tomatoes
1½ teaspoons salt
3 tablespoons olive oil
1 medium onion, finely diced
1 large zucchini or 2 medium yellow pattypan
   (sunburst) squashes, peeled and shredded
1 large carrot, peeled and shredded
2 teaspoons balsamic vinegar
1 teaspoon herbes de Provence
½ cup plus 2 tablespoons chicken broth
½ cup couscous
6 slices Italian prosciutto, finely diced
3 lettuce leaves, cut into thin strips
Fresh parsley leaves, garlic flowers,
   or borage blossoms for garnish

1 • Set a tomato on its stem end. With a sharp paring knife, carve it into a basket by removing 2 wedges from the top half of the tomato, being careful to leave a ½-inch "handle" between them.

2 • With a melon baller, scoop out the seeds and most of pulp from the bottom portion and handle of the tomato basket, leaving a ¼-inch shell. Sprinkle each basket with a little of the salt. Set aside. Dice enough pulp to obtain ¼ cup. Refrigerate the remaining pulp for later use.

3 • In a large skillet, heat 2 tablespoons of the olive oil over medium-high heat. Cook the onion, stirring occasionally, until golden brown, 8 to 10 minutes. Add the zucchini, carrot, and reserved tomato pulp. Reduce heat to medium. Cover and cook for 10 minutes. Add the balsamic vinegar, herbes de Provence, and ¼ teaspoon of the salt. Cook, uncovered, until most of the liquid has evaporated, 10 to 12 minutes. Set aside.

4 • In a medium saucepan over medium-high heat, combine the broth with the remaining olive oil and remaining salt. Bring to a boil. Add the couscous in a stream. Stir once. Remove from the heat. Cover and let stand until the couscous is tender, 12 to 15 minutes. Let cool.

5 • Reserve ¼ cup of the cooked vegetables. In a large bowl, combine the remaining vegetables with the couscous and the diced prosciutto. Set aside.

6 • Line a serving platter with shredded lettuce. With a paper towel, pat dry the inside of each tomato basket. Spoon ½ to ¾ cup of the couscous mixture into each basket. Garnish with parsley or edible flowers. Set the tomatoes on the bed of lettuce. Spoon the reserved vegetables around the base of the tomatoes. Serve at room temperature.

COUSCOUS–PARSLEY SALAD
WITH PRESERVED LEMON

Lebanese tabbouleh incorporates bulgur wheat with generous amounts of parsley, mint, and lemon juice. My North African adaptation substitutes couscous for the bulgur wheat and uses a unique Moroccan condiment, preserved lemon.

Serves 4

¼ cup couscous

¼ cup water

2 tablespoons fresh lemon juice

2 teaspoons olive oil

40 sprigs fresh flat-leaf parsley, finely chopped (about ¼ cup)

30 fresh mint leaves, finely chopped (about 2 tablespoons)

2 teaspoons finely diced Moroccan Preserved Lemon rind (page 23)

1 tablespoon pine nuts, toasted (see page 20)

¾ teaspoon salt

⅛ teaspoon freshly ground pepper

1 small tomato, peeled, seeded (see page 22), and diced

2 Belgian endives, separated into leaves, for scooping

1 • In a medium bowl, combine the couscous with the water and lemon juice. Let stand 1 hour.

2 • To the couscous add the olive oil, parsley, mint, preserved lemon rind, pine nuts, salt, and pepper. Mound the couscous in the center of a serving platter. Top with the diced tomato. Surround the base with endive leaves. Serve at room temperature.

VIETNAMESE COUSCOUS SALAD

I first became acquainted with Vietnamese food and the versatile and pungent nuoc mam fish sauce while growing up in Casablanca, where my friends and I used to patronize several popular Vietnamese restaurants. This inspired me to combine the flavors of Vietnam with those of my native North Africa.

Serves 4 to 6

DRESSING
1 garlic clove, minced
1 teaspoon minced gingerroot
6 tablespoons fresh lime juice
3 tablespoons sugar
2 tablespoons peanut oil
2 tablespoons *nuoc mam* (see Note)
1 teaspoon hot pepper flakes (optional)

SALAD
1⅓ cups boiling water
1 extra-large fish bouillon cube (see Note)
1 tablespoon peanut oil
1 cup couscous
20 sprigs fresh cilantro, finely chopped
    (about 2 tablespoons)
30 fresh mint leaves, finely chopped
    (about 2 tablespoons)
½ cup (about 4 ounces) salted,
    dry-roasted peanuts, coarsely chopped
2 medium carrots, peeled and shredded
1 medium cucumber, peeled, seeded, and shredded
6 green onions, green tops included, finely sliced
½ Napa (Chinese) cabbage, finely shredded
8 ounces medium shrimp, cooked (see Note),
    and coarsely chopped
Fresh cilantro leaves for garnish
Fresh mint leaves for garnish

1 • **To make the dressing:** In a pint jar, combine the garlic, gingerroot, lime juice, sugar, peanut oil, *nuoc mam,* and hot pepper flakes, if using. Shake well. Set aside.

2 • **To make the salad:** In a medium saucepan over medium heat, bring the water, bouillon cube, and peanut oil to a boil. Add the couscous in a stream. Remove from the heat. Stir once. Cover and let stand until the couscous is tender, 12 to 15 minutes. Set aside to cool. Mix with half of the cilantro, half of the mint, and half of the peanuts.

3 • In a large bowl, combine the carrots, cucumber, onions, cabbage, and remaining cilantro and mint. Add the dressing and toss thoroughly.

4 • Spoon equal portions of couscous onto 6 dinner plates. Top with the vegetable mixture and the shrimp. Garnish with the remaining peanuts, cilantro, and mint leaves. Serve at room temperature.

NOTE: *To cook the shrimp, rinse them under running water. In a medium saucepan, bring 4 cups water and 2 bay leaves to a boil. Add the shrimp, and cook until they are just pink, 4 to 5 minutes. Drain and let cool. Discard the cooking liquid and bay leaves. Shell and devein the shrimp.*

Nuoc mam and fish bouillon cubes are available in Asian markets and in specialty food stores.

MAIN COURSES

COUSCOUS MEATLOAF CHERMOULA

Chermoula is a traditional Moroccan marinade redolent of cilantro, cumin, and paprika. I use it with meat, seafood, or vegetables. Here, combined with couscous, chermoula lends an exotic North African touch to something that is quintessentially North American.

Serves 8

3 tablespoons olive oil

1 medium onion, finely diced

1 red bell pepper, seeded and finely diced

3 garlic cloves, minced

One 16-ounce can tomato sauce

36 sprigs fresh cilantro, minced (about ½ cup)

4 teaspoons ground cumin

4 teaspoons sweet Hungarian paprika

1 teaspoon salt

½ teaspoon freshly ground pepper

2 teaspoons sugar

One 14¼-ounce can beef broth

¾ cup couscous

1 pound ground lamb

1 pound ground sirloin

2 eggs, lightly beaten

1 beef bouillon cube, crushed

3 medium tomatoes, peeled, seeded (see page 22), and coarsely chopped

1 • In a medium skillet, heat the olive oil over medium heat. Cook the onion, pepper, and garlic, stirring occasionally, until the onion turns golden, 4 to 5 minutes. Transfer to a medium bowl and set aside.

2 • In a medium saucepan over medium heat, combine the tomato sauce, cilantro, cumin, paprika, salt, pepper, and sugar. Cook, stirring, until the tomato sauce begins to bubble, 4 to 5 minutes.

Remove from the heat. Add half of the *chermoula* sauce to the onion-pepper mixture. Keep the remaining sauce in the pan. Set aside.

3 • Meanwhile, in a medium saucepan, bring 1 cup of the broth to a boil. Add the couscous in a stream. Stir once. Remove from the heat. Cover and let stand until couscous is tender, 12 to 15 minutes. Set aside.

4 • Preheat the oven to 350 degrees F. Lightly oil a 6-cup ring mold. In a large bowl, combine the couscous with the ground lamb, ground sirloin, onion-pepper mixture, and eggs. Mix with your hands to break up any lumps, and spoon into the mold. Smooth off the top with a spatula. Set the mold within a larger baking pan, to catch any juice that boils over. Bake until firm, about 1 hour. Remove from the oven and let the meatloaf rest 10 minutes. Invert on a serving platter.

5 • Meanwhile, over medium heat, combine the remaining *chermoula* sauce with the remaining broth, the crushed bouillon cube, and chopped tomatoes. Cook until the sauce thickens somewhat, 6 to 8 minutes. Spoon some *chermoula* sauce over the meatloaf, and serve with extra *chermoula* on the side.

BOEUF BOURGUIGNON WITH MUSHROOM COUSCOUS

The boeuf bourguignon, *simmered in a rich, red wine sauce, will develop a deeper flavor if prepared a day ahead. When I have the time, I like to use my Crock-Pot, letting the beef simmer all day long on low heat.*

Serves 6

2 pounds boneless beef round roast
3 tablespoons flour
½ teaspoon salt
¼ teaspoon freshly ground pepper
4 ounces salt pork, rind removed
2 medium carrots, peeled and thinly sliced
2 medium onions, finely diced
5 tablespoons olive oil
2¼ cups red Burgundy wine
3¼ cups beef broth
2 bay leaves
2 garlic cloves, slivered
2 ribs celery, finely diced
1½ teaspoons herbes de Provence
24 pearl onions
1 pound small button mushrooms, cleaned and dried
1 red bell pepper, seeded and finely diced
¾ cup couscous
Fresh parsley for garnish

1 • Trim and cut the beef into 1½-by-½-inch pieces. In a paper or plastic bag, combine the flour, salt, and pepper. Add the beef to the bag, and shake to coat. Set aside.

2 • Cube the salt pork. In a heavy, medium non-reactive pan over medium-high heat, cook until browned, 6 to 8 minutes. With a slotted spoon, transfer to a small bowl and set aside.

3 • To the same pan, add the carrots and half of the diced onions. Cook, stirring occasionally, until the vegetables are lightly browned, 8 to 10 minutes. With a slotted spoon, transfer them to a small bowl and set aside.

4 • To the same pan over medium-high heat, add 2 tablespoons of the olive oil. Cook the beef in batches, until browned on all sides, 6 to 8 minutes. Return the beef to the pan. Add the wine, 2¼ cups of the beef broth, the bay leaves, garlic, celery, and herbes de Provence. Reduce heat to medium. Cover and cook until the beef is tender, 1¼ to 1½ hours. Do not allow the liquid to cook away. Add additional broth, if necessary.

(continued)

5 • Meanwhile, in a small saucepan filled with boiling water, blanch the pearl onions for 1 minute. Drain and let cool. Peel the onions and set aside.

6 • Cut the caps off of 12 mushrooms and set aside. Finely dice the stems along with the remaining mushrooms. Set aside.

7 • When the beef is tender, add the reserved salt pork, pearl onions, and mushroom caps. Cook until the mushroom caps are tender, 15 to 20 minutes. Discard the bay leaves. Keep the stew warm until ready to serve.

8 • In a medium skillet over medium-high heat, heat 2 tablespoons of the olive oil. Cook the remaining diced onion and the bell pepper, stirring occasionally, until the onion turns golden, 4 to 5 minutes. Add the diced mushrooms, and cook until tender, 3 to 4 minutes. Season with additional salt and pepper. Set aside.

9 • To prepare the couscous, in a medium saucepan over medium heat, bring the remaining cup of beef broth and tablespoon of olive oil to a boil. Add the couscous in a stream. Stir once. Remove from the heat. Cover and let stand until couscous is tender, 12 to 15 minutes. Combine the couscous with the mushroom-vegetable mixture.

10 • Lightly oil a 6-cup ring mold. Spoon the couscous into the mold and pat down firmly. Invert the mold onto a large serving platter. With a slotted spoon, transfer the beef to the center of the ring. Spoon half of the wine sauce over the beef. Arrange the pearl onions and mushroom caps around the base of the ring. Garnish with parsley. Serve with the remaining sauce on the side.

INDONESIAN COUSCOUS STIR-FRY

Friends who lived in both North Africa and the Far East often substitute couscous for rice in this popular Indonesian stir-fry called nasi goreng. *It is usually served with an assortment of pickled vegetables. If you prefer, use chicken, pork, beef, or shrimp instead of ham.*

Serves 6

1 medium cucumber, peeled and thinly sliced
2 tablespoons rice vinegar
2 tablespoons peanut oil
2 eggs, lightly beaten
1½ cups chicken broth
1¼ cups couscous
1 small onion, quartered
3 garlic cloves, minced
One ½-inch piece gingerroot, peeled
1 tablespoon *nuoc mam* or *nam pla* (see Note),
   Sambal manis (see Note), **Thai hot sauce,**
   or Tabasco sauce to taste
1 cup (about 6 ounces) cubed ham
½ cup frozen peas or cut-up green beans
1 tablespoon oyster sauce (see Note)
1 tablespoon sweet soy sauce (see Note)
4 green onions, white parts only, finely sliced
2 tablespoons water
4 leaves romaine lettuce, cut into thin strips

1 • Drain the cucumber well. In a medium bowl, combine it with the rice vinegar. Marinate 30 minutes and drain. Set aside.

2 • In a medium skillet, heat 2 teaspoons of the peanut oil over medium heat. Add the eggs, and roll the pan to obtain a thin omelet. Cook until the eggs are set, 2 to 3 minutes. Slide the omelet onto a dinner plate. Let cool. Cut into strips ¼ inch by 2 inches. Set aside.

3 • In a medium saucepan over medium heat, bring the broth to a boil. Add the couscous in a stream. Stir once. Remove from the heat. Cover and let stand until the couscous is tender, 12 to 15 minutes. Fluff with a fork. Set aside.

4 • In a blender or food processor, purée the onion, garlic, gingerroot, *nuoc mam*, and hot sauce, if using. Set aside.

5 • In a large wok or nonstick skillet over medium-high heat, warm the remaining peanut oil. Add the onion mixture. Cook, stirring, until the oil begins to foam, 4 to 5 minutes. Add the ham, couscous, peas, oyster sauce, soy sauce, half of the green onions, and the water. With two spatulas, toss all the ingredients until they are coated with the sauce. Heat through, 3 to 4 minutes. Mound in the center of the serving platter. Surround with the lettuce and drained cucumber slices. Garnish with remaining green onions and omelet strips, and serve.

NOTE: *Indonesian sambal manis, nuoc mam (Vietnamese fish sauce), nam pla (Thai fish sauce), Thai hot sauce, sweet soy sauce, and oyster sauce are available in Asian markets and specialty markets.*

LETTUCE-WRAPPED COUSCOUS TERRINE WITH DILLED SHRIMP AND YOGURT SAUCE

You will find this refreshing, light terrine easier to slice after it is chilled. It is an ideal dish for a summer buffet luncheon.

Serves 6 to 8

1 large head romaine lettuce
3 tablespoons olive oil
1 medium onion, finely diced
1 red bell pepper, seeded and finely diced
1 small fennel bulb, trimmed and finely diced
8 ounces cooked baby shrimp, coarsely chopped
2 teaspoons Moroccan Preserved Lemon rind (page 23)
1 teaspoon salt
1/8 teaspoon freshly ground pepper
12 sprigs dill, finely minced (about 2 tablespoons)
Two 7-gram packets (about 2 teaspoons) plain gelatin
1 1/3 cups chicken broth
1 cup couscous
1/4 cup plain yogurt
1/4 cup sour cream
1 garlic clove, minced
2 tablespoons fresh lemon juice

1 • Lightly oil a 9-by-5-by-3-inch loaf pan. Set aside. Pull off 12 large outer green leaves from the head of romaine lettuce. With a sharp knife, remove a 2- to 3-inch V-shaped wedge from the tough white center rib of each leaf.

2 • In a large saucepan filled with boiling water, blanch the leaves until they wilt, 30 to 40 seconds. With tongs, transfer them to a bowl filled with cold water. This will stop the cooking process and preserve the green color. Drain. Transfer the leaves to a baking sheet covered with paper towels. Pat dry, and line the sides and bottom of the loaf pan with the blanched leaves, letting them hang 1 to 2 inches over the edge of the pan. Set aside.

3 • In a large skillet over medium-high heat, heat 2 tablespoons of the olive oil. Cook the onion, pepper, and fennel, stirring occasionally, until the onion is golden, 5 to 6 minutes. Add the shrimp, preserved lemon rind, half of the salt, and the pepper. Cook, stirring, until the shrimp is well coated, 2 to 3 minutes. Stir in 1 tablespoon of the dill. Reserve 1 cup of the shrimp mixture for garnish, and refrigerate.

4 • In a small saucepan, sprinkle the gelatin into 1/3 cup of the broth. Let stand 1 minute. Set the pan over low heat. Cook, stirring, until the gelatin is completely dissolved, 2 to 3 minutes. Set aside.

(continued)

5 • In a medium saucepan over medium-high heat, bring the remaining 1 cup of broth and the remaining salt to a boil. Add the couscous in a stream. Remove from the heat. Add the gelatin mixture and stir. Cover and let stand until couscous is tender, 12 to 15 minutes.

6 • Spoon half of the couscous into the bottom of the lettuce-lined pan. Pat down evenly. Cover with the remaining shrimp mixture (not the garnish). Pat down the remaining couscous over the shrimp. Fold the lettuce leaves over the couscous. Refrigerate at least 2 hours.

7 • Meanwhile, make the yogurt sauce. In a medium bowl combine the yogurt, sour cream, garlic, lemon juice, and remaining tablespoon of dill.

8 • Invert the terrine on a serving platter. Cut 3 or 4 lettuce leaves into thin ribbons and use them as garnish around the loaf. Top with the refrigerated shrimp mixture. Serve with yogurt sauce on the side.

COUSCOUS SALMON PATTIES WITH GREEN PEA AND PINE NUT SAUCE

The tanginess of the capers offsets the delicate green pea sauce that tops these delicious salmon patties.

Serves 4

¼ cup couscous
¼ cup water
One 14¾-ounce can salmon
2 eggs, lightly beaten
2 tablespoons capers, drained
1 teaspoon dry mustard
20 sprigs fresh dill, minced (about 2 tablespoons)
1 teaspoon salt
¼ teaspoon freshly ground pepper
1 medium onion, finely diced
2 tablespoons fresh lemon juice
2 tablespoons butter
4 ounces Chinese pea pods, stringed
1⅓ cups (8 ounces) frozen petite peas
2 tablespoons pine nuts, toasted (see page 20)
1 cup chicken broth
Oil for frying
Lemon wedges for serving

1 • In a small bowl, combine the couscous with the water. Let stand until the water is absorbed, 8 to 10 minutes. Set aside.

2 • Discard salmon skin and bones. In a medium bowl, break up the salmon with a fork. Combine it with the couscous, eggs, capers, mustard, half of the dill, the salt, pepper, half of the onion, and the lemon juice. Blend thoroughly. Refrigerate for 30 minutes.

3 • Meanwhile, in a medium skillet over medium-high heat, melt the butter. Cook the Chinese pea pods, stirring occasionally until they glisten, 1 to 2 minutes. With a slotted spoon, transfer the pods to a small plate. Set aside.

4 • In the same pan, cook the remaining onion, stirring occasionally, until golden, 4 to 5 minutes. Add the petite peas. Cook, stirring, until the peas are tender, 1 to 2 minutes. Let cool.

5 • In a blender, combine the onion, petite peas, pine nuts, and broth. Process until smooth and transfer to a small saucepan over medium heat. Cook until the sauce thickens somewhat, 12 to 15 minutes. Stir in the remaining dill. Keep warm.

6 • In a large skillet, pour oil to depth of ½ inch. Heat the oil over medium-high heat until a pinch of the salmon mixture sizzles instantly. Using your hands, shape ¼ cup increments of the salmon mixture into patties 3½ inches in diameter and ¾ inch thick. Set the patties in the skillet. Cook until golden brown, 5 to 6 minutes on each side. Transfer to a plate lined with paper towels to drain.

7 • Spoon ½ cup of green pea and pine nut sauce onto each of 4 dinner plates and set a salmon patty on each. Garnish with additional sauce and pea pods. Serve with lemon wedges.

COUSCOUS FRITTERS WITH
FRESH CORN AND TOMATO SALSA

Prepare this dish at the peak of the corn and tomato season to take advantage of the sweetest, ripest ingredients for the salsa.

Serves 4

2 large, ripe tomatoes, peeled, seeded (see page 20),
   finely diced, and drained
2 ears sweet corn, shucked and cooked
   (about 1½ cups kernels)
15 sprigs fresh cilantro, finely chopped
   (about 1½ tablespoons)
2 tablespoons finely diced onion
1 teaspoon fresh lime juice
¾ teaspoon ground cumin
1 tablespoon ketchup
¾ teaspoon salt
⅔ cup broth
1 teaspoon chili powder
1 tablespoon butter
½ cup couscous
1 egg, lightly beaten
Vegetable oil for frying
8 ounces turkey sausage or pork sausage,
   casing removed

1 • In a medium bowl, combine the tomatoes, corn, half of the cilantro, the onion, lime juice, ¼ teaspoon of the cumin, the ketchup, and salt. Set aside.

2 • Prepare the fritters: In a medium saucepan over medium-high heat, combine the broth, chili powder, butter, and remaining salt. Bring to a boil. Add the couscous in a stream. Stir once. Cover and remove from the heat. Set aside until the couscous is tender, 12 to 15 minutes. Transfer to a medium bowl and combine with the egg.

3 • Preheat the oven to 200 degrees F. In a medium skillet over medium-high heat, pour vegetable oil to a depth of ½ inch. Heat until a pinch of couscous sizzles instantly. Place the couscous mixture, in ⅓ cup increments, into the skillet. With a spatula, flatten into croquettes 3 to 3½ inches in diameter. Fry until golden brown, 6 to 8 minutes on each side. Transfer to a plate lined with paper towels to drain. Keep warm in the oven.

4 • In another medium skillet over medium heat, cook the sausage, breaking it up with a fork, until thoroughly cooked, 6 to 8 minutes. With the spatula, transfer the meat to a plate lined with paper towels to drain. Set aside.

5 • Spoon some of the salsa onto 4 individual dinner plates. Set a fritter in the center of each plate. Top with equal portions of sausage and additional salsa. Garnish with the remaining cilantro leaves and serve.

COUSCOUS MARINARA WITH SWEET ITALIAN SAUSAGE

The flavor of the marinara sauce in this recipe will be even more intense if made a day or two ahead.

Serves 4

MARINARA SAUCE
1 tablespoon olive oil
3 garlic cloves, peeled
One 28-ounce can diced Italian plum tomatoes
One 6-ounce can tomato paste with roasted garlic
3 cups water
1 heaping teaspoon dried oregano leaves
1 tablespoon dark brown sugar
1 teaspoon salt
½ teaspoon freshly ground pepper
1 pound sweet Italian sausage

COUSCOUS
3 cups water
½ teaspoon salt
2 teaspoons olive oil
1 cup plus 2 tablespoons couscous
2 eggs, beaten
¼ cup grated Parmesan cheese, plus extra for serving
1 ounce dried diced porcini mushrooms (see Note)
15 large fresh basil leaves, minced
   (about 3 tablespoons), plus 6 whole fresh basil
   leaves for garnish

1 • To make the sauce: In a large cast-iron or nonreactive pan, heat the olive oil over medium-high heat. Cook the garlic, stirring occasionally, until golden, 2 to 3 minutes. With a slotted spoon, discard the garlic. Reduce heat to medium-low. Add the tomatoes, tomato paste, water, oregano, brown sugar, salt, pepper, and sausage. Cook covered, until sausage is well done, 1½ to 2 hours. Uncover, and cook until the sauce reduces by half, 50 minutes to 1 hour. Skim off the fat. Keep warm.

2 • Meanwhile, make the couscous: In a medium saucepan, bring 1½ cups of the water, the salt, and olive oil to a boil. Add the couscous in a stream. Stir once. Remove from heat. Cover and let stand until the couscous is tender, 12 to 15 minutes. Set aside.

3 • In a medium bowl, combine the eggs, remaining 1½ cups water, the cheese, mushrooms, and chopped basil. Add the cooked couscous, and mix thoroughly.

4 • Lightly grease a round, 2-quart baking dish or a soufflé dish. Add the couscous mixture. Cover tightly with foil. Place on a rack inside a large pan filled with lightly simmering water. The water should come a third of the way up the sides of the dish. Cover and cook over low to medium-low heat until the couscous sets, $1\frac{1}{2}$ to $1\frac{3}{4}$ hours. Add more hot water to the pan during cooking time, if necessary.

5 • With a slotted spoon, remove the sausages from the tomato sauce. Slice each sausage on the diagonal. Keep warm.

6 • Unmold the couscous onto a serving platter. Top with some of the sauce and surround with slices of sausage. Garnish with fresh basil leaves. Serve with extra marinara sauce and Parmesan cheese on the side.

NOTE: *Packages of dried diced porcini mushrooms are available in the produce section of some large supermakets, and in specialty markets.*

COUSCOUS GUMBO

Okra, like couscous, originated in Africa, where it is still known as "gombo." So pairing the two ingredients seemed only natural. Filé, a powder made from dried ground sassafras leaves, is essential for thickening the sauce.

Serves 6

½ cup vegetable oil

1 pound okra, trimmed and cut into ½-inch pieces

2 medium onions, finely diced (about 2 cups)

½ red bell pepper, seeded and finely diced

2 ears of corn, shucked (about 1½ cup kernels)

1 pound chicken legs and thighs

2 tablespoons flour

One 14¾-ounce can Italian plum tomatoes (do not drain)

5 garlic cloves, minced

3¼ cups chicken broth

2 bay leaves

1 teaspoon salt

¼ teaspoon cayenne pepper

1 teaspoon filé powder (see Note)

8 ounces Cajun-style andouille sausage, cut into ¼-inch slices

1 tablespoon Worcestershire sauce

1 cup couscous

Fresh parsley leaves for garnish

Tabasco sauce (optional)

1 • In a heavy skillet over medium-high heat, heat 2 tablespoons of the oil. Cook the okra, stirring occasionally, until no longer slippery, 15 to 20 minutes. With a slotted spoon, transfer the okra to a bowl. Set aside.

2 • In the same skillet, cook the onions, stirring occasionally until browned, 8 to 10 minutes. With a slotted spoon, add the onions to the okra. Set aside.

3 • Add 1 tablespoon of the oil to the skillet. Cook the bell pepper and corn kernels, stirring occasionally, until the pepper turns soft, 4 to 5 minutes. With a slotted spoon, transfer the vegetables to a small bowl. Keep warm.

4 • If necessary, add another tablespoon of the oil to the skillet. Cook the chicken, turning with tongs until browned on all sides, 6 to 8 minutes. Transfer to a bowl and set aside.

5 • Reduce heat to medium. In the same skillet, measure 3 tablespoons of the oil. Add the flour. Cook, stirring continuously, until the flour turns light brown, 6 to 8 minutes. Add the tomatoes. Cook, stirring, until the mixture thickens somewhat, 2 to 3 minutes. Add the reserved okra, onions, chicken, the garlic, 2 cups of the broth, the bay leaves, half of the salt and cayenne pepper, and the filé powder. Cook, covered, until the chicken is tender, 30 to 35 minutes.

(continued)

6 • Add the andouille sausage and Worcestershire sauce. Cook, covered, until the sausage is tender, 10 to 15 minutes. Discard the bay leaves.

7 • Meanwhile, prepare the couscous. In a medium saucepan, bring the remaining 1¼ cups broth, 1 tablespoon of the oil, and the remaining salt and cayenne pepper to a boil. Add the couscous in a stream. Stir once. Remove from the heat. Cover and let stand until couscous is tender, 12 to 15 minutes. In a medium bowl, combine the couscous with the reserved bell pepper and corn mixture.

8 • Gently pack equal amounts of couscous into 6 generously greased 6-ounce ramekins. Unmold into the centers of 6 warm, shallow soup plates. Spoon gumbo around the couscous. Garnish with parsley leaves. Serve with Tabasco sauce on the side.

NOTE: *Filé powder is available in specialty food stores.*

COUSCOUS PAELLA

Moorish and Andalusian cultures reunite when couscous takes the place of rice in one of southern Spain's most famous dishes.

Serves 4

4 tablespoons olive oil

½ red bell pepper, seeded and cut into ¼-inch strips

2 medium onions, finely diced

4 chicken legs

1 chicken sausage or turkey sausage, thinly sliced

One 14½-ounce can diced tomatoes

10 threads Spanish saffron (see page 22)

3 garlic cloves, minced

12 littleneck clams, scrubbed

12 mussels, byssal threads removed
  (see Note page 44)

1 cup chicken or fish broth (see Note)

One 14¼-ounce can artichoke hearts,
  drained and rinsed

½ cup frozen petite peas

8 medium shrimp, shelled and deveined

1 cup couscous

Lemon wedges for garnish

1 • In a large skillet or paella pan over medium-high heat, warm the olive oil. Add the pepper strips. Cook, stirring, until tender, 3 to 4 to minutes. With a slotted spoon, transfer the strips to a small bowl. Cover and set aside.

2 • Preheat the oven to 200 degrees F. To the same skillet, add the onions. Cook, stirring until they wilt, 3 to 4 minutes. Add the chicken legs. Cook, turning, until lightly browned on all sides, 3 to 4 minutes. Add the sausage, tomatoes, saffron, and garlic. Reduce the heat to medium. Cover and cook until the chicken is tender, 30 to 35 minutes. With a slotted spoon, transfer the chicken legs to an oven-proof dish and keep warm in the oven. Keep the sausage-tomato mixture simmering on the stove.

3 • Meanwhile, in a small saucepan over high heat, place the clams and the mussels. Cook, covered, until the shellfish open, 6 to 8 minutes. Discard any shellfish that do not open. With a slotted spoon, transfer the shellfish to a steamer or a colander set over gently simmering water, and keep warm.

4 • Pour the shellfish cooking liquid into a large measuring container. Add enough broth to make 1½ cups, and add to the skillet. Add the artichoke hearts, peas, and shrimp. Cover and cook until heated through, 2 to 3 minutes. Sprinkle the couscous evenly over the dish. Remove from the heat. Cover and let stand until the couscous is tender, 12 to 15 minutes. Using tongs, arrange the reserved chicken legs, shellfish, and pepper strips over the couscous. Garnish with lemon wedges.

NOTE : *Fish bouillon cubes are available in Asian and Mexican markets and in specialty food stores.*

COUSCOUS CHICKEN FRICASSÉE WITH TARRAGON

Blanquette de poulet, a fricassée of chicken in a lemony tarragon sauce, is traditionally served on rice, but I prefer to serve it over a bed of light and fluffy couscous.

Serves 4

4 tablespoons butter
2 ribs celery, cut into 1-inch-long matchsticks
2 carrots, cut into 1-inch-long matchsticks
1 medium leek, green leaves removed,
    cut into 1-inch-long matchsticks
8 ounces small button mushroom caps
2 tablespoons flour
¼ teaspoon freshly ground pepper
4 small boneless chicken breasts, cubed
2¼ cups chicken broth
1 cup dry white wine
1½ teaspoons dried tarragon leaves
1 bay leaf
8 roasted garlic cloves (see page 22), mashed
2 egg yolks, lightly beaten
1 tablespoon fresh lemon juice
1 teaspoon salt
¾ cup couscous
½ cup frozen petite peas

1 • In a large skillet or a medium saucepan, over medium-high heat, warm 2 tablespoons of the butter. Cook the celery, carrots, and leek, stirring occasionally until the leek is translucent, 4 to 5 minutes. With a slotted spoon, transfer the vegetables to a small bowl. Set aside.

2 • To the same skillet, add the mushrooms. Cook, stirring, until tender, 2 to 3 minutes. With a slotted spoon, transfer to a small bowl. Set aside.

3 • Place the flour and pepper in a paper bag. Add the chicken, shake well to coat and add to the skillet. Cook, turning, until lightly browned on all sides, 4 to 5 minutes. Add 1½ cups of the broth, half of the wine, half of the tarragon, and the bay leaf. Cook, stirring occasionally, until the chicken is tender, 8 to 10 minutes. With a slotted spoon, transfer the chicken to a bowl. Discard the bay leaf. Set aside chicken. Reduce heat to low.

4 • In a small bowl, beat the garlic with the egg yolks and lemon juice. Remove the skillet from the heat and whisk in the egg-lemon mixture. Return to the heat, and whisk continuously until the sauce thickens to the consistency of light custard. Return the reserved chicken and the reserved vegetables to the skillet. Stir until heated through. Do not allow the sauce to boil or it may curdle.

5 • Meanwhile, in a medium saucepan, bring the remaining broth, wine, butter, tarragon, and the salt to a boil. Add the couscous and the peas in a stream. Stir once. Remove from the heat. Cover and let stand until the couscous is tender, 12 to 15 minutes. Fluff with a fork. Set aside.

6 • Gently pack equal amounts of couscous into 4 well-greased 6-ounce ramekins. Invert onto warm dinner plates. Arrange the chicken and vegetables over and around the couscous and serve.

COUSCOUS TONNATO WITH FRIED CAPER BUDS

Vittello tonnato is a specialty of the Lombardy region of Italy. It inspired me to create this pork tenderloin and couscous adaptation, which I like to serve for an alfresco buffet.

Serves 4

3 tablespoons finely diced sun-dried tomatoes
¼ cup white wine vinegar
2 teaspoons sugar
1 tablespoon cracked black peppercorns
1¼ pounds boneless pork tenderloin
1 cup water
1 fish bouillon cube (see Note)
3 tablespoons olive oil
¾ cup couscous
One 4-ounce jar capers, drained
6 anchovy fillets in olive oil, drained
One 6-ounce can tuna in oil (preferably olive oil)
1 tablespoon fresh lemon juice
¼ cup plain yogurt
3 tablespoons light cream
Vegetable oil for frying

1 • In a small bowl, combine the sun-dried tomatoes, vinegar, and sugar. Set aside.

2 • Preheat the broiler. Sprinkle a work surface with the cracked peppercorns. Roll the tenderloin in the peppercorns to coat evenly. Place on a rack set over a small roasting pan, 4 inches from the broiler. Cook, turning once or twice, 15 to 18 minutes. The outside should be well done, while the inside should remain slightly pink. Let stand 15 minutes. Cut into ⅛-inch-thick slices. Set aside.

3 • In a medium saucepan, bring the water, bouillon cube, and 1 tablespoon of olive oil to a boil. Add the couscous in a stream. Stir once. Remove from heat.

Cover and let stand until couscous is tender, 12 to 15 minutes. Transfer the couscous to a medium bowl. Combine with 1 tablespoon of the capers. Set aside.

4 • To prepare the sauce: In a blender combine the anchovies, tuna, lemon juice, yogurt, remaining olive oil, and the cream. Blend until smooth. Mix half the sauce with the couscous. Set the rest aside.

5 • Meanwhile, in a small saucepan or skillet over high heat, pour vegetable oil to a depth of ½ inch and heat it to the smoking stage. Dry the remaining capers with paper towels. Drop the capers into the hot oil, and fry until they open like tiny flower buds, about 30 to 40 seconds. (Beware of splattering.) With a slotted spoon, transfer to a plate lined with paper towels to drain. Set aside.

6 • Drain the diced sun-dried tomatoes and place equal portions into 4 small bowls or ramekins. Into each bowl, spoon ⅔ cup of couscous. Pat down evenly. Invert each ramekin, off center, on a dinner plate. Arrange the pork slices in a fan-shaped pattern on one side of the plate. Spoon remaining *tonnato* sauce over the pork. Garnish with fried capers and additional pepper, if desired. Serve chilled or at room temperature.

NOTE: *Fish bouillon cubes are available in Asian and Mexican markets and in specialty food stores.*

COUSCOUS KIEV

Make sure you refrigerate these stuffed chicken breasts at least one hour before baking. Serve them hot, on a bed of braised cabbage, or chilled and thinly sliced, as you would a cold cut.

Serves 6

6 large skinless, boneless chicken breasts
1 cup chicken broth
8 tablespoons (1 stick) butter
1 teaspoon salt
¾ cup couscous
10 roasted garlic cloves (see page 22), mashed
3 tablespoons chopped fresh chives
1 egg, well beaten
½ teaspoon freshly ground pepper
¾ cup unseasoned bread crumbs

1 • On a flat work surface, sandwich each chicken breast between two sheets of plastic wrap. Pound to ¼ inch thick. Set aside.

2 • In a medium saucepan over medium-high heat, bring the broth, 1 tablespoon of the butter, and ½ teaspoon of the salt to a boil. Add the couscous in a stream. Stir once. Remove from the heat. Cover and let stand until the couscous is tender, 12 to 15 minutes. Add the mashed garlic, chives, egg, and half of the pepper. Stir to blend.

3 • In a small saucepan over medium heat, melt the remaining butter. Set aside.

4 • Place equal amounts of couscous in the middle of each chicken breast. Fold over the breast to cover the couscous. Using your hands, cradle and mold each breast into an oblong shape, sealing the chicken to itself.

5 • Place the melted butter in a shallow bowl. In another shallow bowl, mix the bread crumbs with the remaining salt and the pepper. With your hands, liberally coat each breast with butter, then roll in the bread crumb mixture to coat evenly. Transfer to a platter and refrigerate for at least one hour.

6 • Preheat the oven to 350 degrees F. Bake the breasts, basting once with butter, until they turn golden, 40 to 45 minutes. Serve hot or cold.

EGGPLANT TERRINES WITH COUSCOUS, PANCETTA, AND PORTOBELLO MUSHROOMS

The large, purple-skinned, ovoid fruit known as "eggplant" or "aubergine" originated in India. Today, however, it is an integral part of Mediterranean cuisine, especially that of Italy, whose flavors inspired this recipe.

Serves 6

3 large eggplants
Salt for sprinkling
⅓ cup olive oil
3 garlic cloves, minced
10 slices (about 3 ounces) Italian pancetta or bacon,
   finely diced (see Note)
8 ounces portobello mushrooms, finely diced
1 cup chicken broth
¾ cup couscous
1¼ cups (about 5 ounces) coarsely grated
   Asiago cheese
1 egg, well beaten
1¼ teaspoons salt
¼ teaspoon freshly ground pepper
10 medium tomatoes, peeled,
   seeded (see page 22), and diced
10 large fresh basil leaves, finely chopped
   (about 2 tablespoons)

1 • Peel the eggplants. Cut off a quarter-size piece from the blossom end. With the eggplants on end, cut lengthwise into ¼-inch slices. Finely dice several smaller slices to obtain 2 cups. Set aside.

2 • Place the remaining slices on a work surface lined with paper towels. Sprinkle lightly with salt, and "sweat" for 15 minutes. Turn slices over, salt, and sweat for another 15 minutes. Rinse lightly under running water. Pat dry.

3 • Preheat oven on Broil. In a small bowl, mix the olive oil with the garlic. Reserve 2 tablespoons of this mixture. Using a brush, lightly baste both sides of the eggplant slices with the remaining olive oil–garlic mixture. Place the eggplant slices on a baking sheet lined with aluminum foil. Broil until they are lightly browned, 4 to 5 minutes on each side. Remove from the oven, and set aside to cool. Reduce oven temperature to 425 degrees F.

4 • Meanwhile, in a medium skillet over medium-high heat, cook the pancetta, mushroom, and reserved diced eggplant, stirring occasionally, until the eggplant is soft, 8 to 10 minutes. Set aside.

(continued)

5 • In a medium saucepan over medium-high heat, bring the broth and 1 tablespoon of the reserved olive oil–garlic mixture to a boil. Add the couscous in a stream. Stir once. Remove from the heat. Cover and let stand until the couscous is tender, 12 to 15 minutes. Transfer to a bowl, and add the pancetta-mushroom-eggplant mixture, the cheese, egg, 1/2 teaspoon of the salt, and half of the pepper.

6 • Generously grease six 6-ounce ramekins. Line the base and sides of each with broiled eggplant. Trim the edge with a knife. Gently pack each ramekin with about 1/2 cup of the couscous mixture. Cover tightly with foil. Bake until heated through, 18 to 20 minutes.

7 • Meanwhile, prepare the tomato sauce: In a medium skillet over medium-high heat, warm the remaining tablespoon of the reserved olive oil–garlic mixture. Add the tomatoes. Cook, stirring, until the tomatoes soften, 2 to 3 minutes. Season with basil, and the remaining salt and pepper.

8 • To serve, unmold the ramekins onto 6 warm dinner plates. Spoon tomato sauce over and around each terrine and serve.

NOTE: *Pancetta is available in Italian markets or specialty food stores.*

STEAK AND MUSHROOM PIE WITH DOUBLE GLOUCESTER COUSCOUS

I have substituted a layer of couscous mixed with sharp Double Gloucester cheese for the traditional pastry crust in this old English favorite.

Serves 4

32 pearl onions
3 tablespoons flour
¼ teaspoon freshly ground pepper
8 ounces sirloin steak, cut into ½-inch strips
2 tablespoons olive oil
½ cup dry sherry
2 cups beef broth
1 pound mushrooms, stemmed and quartered
1 teaspoon Worcestershire sauce
2 beef bouillon cubes
½ cup frozen peas, thawed
¾ cup couscous
1 egg, lightly beaten
1 cup (about 4 ounces) coarsely shredded Double
   Gloucester cheese
Chopped fresh parsley for garnish

1 • In a small saucepan filled with boiling water, blanch the pearl onions for 30 seconds. Drain and let cool. Peel the onions. Set aside.

2 • In a paper or plastic bag, combine 2 tablespoons of the flour, the pepper, and the meat. Seal and shake until the meat is well coated. Transfer the meat to a bowl and set aside.

3 • In a medium skillet, heat the olive oil over medium-high heat. Add the onions, and cook, stirring, until they turn light brown, 4 to 5 minutes. Add the meat, and cook, stirring, until

browned on all sides, 3 to 4 minutes. Add the sherry and ½ cup of the broth. Reduce the heat to medium. Cover, and cook until the meat is fairly tender, 20 to 25 minutes. Add the mushrooms, Worcestershire sauce, and bouillon cubes. Cover and cook until the mushrooms are tender, 8 to 10 minutes. With a slotted spoon, transfer the meat, onions, and mushrooms to a 2-quart soufflé dish. Set aside. Keep the sauce simmering in the skillet.

4 • In a small bowl, blend ¼ cup of the broth with the remaining flour. Add to the sauce. Cook, stirring, until the sauce thickens, 3 to 4 minutes. Combine it with the meat and vegetables in the soufflé dish and add the peas. Set aside.

5 • In a medium saucepan over medium heat, bring 1 cup of the broth to a boil. Add the couscous in a stream. Stir once. Remove from the heat. Cover and let stand until the couscous is tender, 12 to 15 minutes.

6 • In the meantime, preheat the oven to 425 degrees F. In a medium bowl, blend the remaining ¼ cup of broth, the egg, and the cheese. Stir into the couscous. With a spatula, spread the couscous mixture evenly over the beef and vegetables. Cover tightly with foil. Bake until piping hot, 18 to 20 minutes. Some of the sauce will bubble through the couscous layer. With a spatula, spread it evenly over the couscous. Garnish with parsley and serve.

COUSCOUS ALLA MILANESE WITH ASPARAGUS

For this dish, I sauté the couscous in a little butter in the same way I would sauté rice when making a risotto. I recommend a generous sprinkling of fresh lemon juice just before serving to heighten the flavor.

Serves 4

3 tablespoons butter
8 ounces fresh asparagus, cut into 1-inch pieces
3 shallots, minced
1 cup couscous
⅓ cup dry white wine
1½ cups chicken broth
8 threads Spanish saffron (see page 22)
¼ teaspoon freshly ground white pepper
1 cup (about 4 ounces) coarsely shredded Asiago cheese
Lemon wedges for serving

1 • Preheat the oven to 350 degrees F. In a heavy saucepan over medium-high heat, warm 2 tablespoons of the butter. Cook the asparagus, stirring occasionally, until tender, 4 to 5 minutes. Remove from the heat and keep warm.

2 • To the same skillet over medium-high heat, add the shallots. Cook, stirring until they turn golden, 3 to 4 minutes. Add the couscous, and cook, stirring, until lightly toasted, 2 to 3 minutes.

3 • In a medium saucepan, combine the wine, 1 cup of the broth, the saffron, and the pepper. Bring to a boil. Add the shallot-couscous mixture. Stir once. Remove from the heat. Cover and let stand until the couscous is tender, 12 to 15 minutes. Stir in the cheese and the remaining butter.

4 • Preheat the oven to 200 degrees F. Transfer couscous to a 2-quart baking dish. Pour the remaining broth over the couscous. Cover tightly with foil, and bake until the cheese melts, 5 to 6 minutes. Stir to blend. Divide the couscous among 4 shallow soup plates. Top with equal portions of asparagus. Sprinkle with lemon juice, and serve with a lemon wedge on the side.

CURRIED COUSCOUS CROQUETTES
WITH RIBBONED VEGETABLES

Serve Curried Couscous Croquettes on their own for a light supper, or as an accompaniment to roasted meats.

Serves 6 (makes about 20 croquettes)

½ cup couscous
½ cup water
4 medium carrots, peeled
3 medium zucchini (do not peel)
1 small onion
4 ounces broccoli florets
3 tablespoons olive oil
1½ tablespoons curry powder
¼ cup walnut pieces
2 garlic cloves, minced
2 eggs, well beaten
6 tablespoons self-rising flour
1 cup light cream
¾ teaspoon salt
¼ teaspoon freshly ground pepper
Vegetable oil for frying

1 • In a medium bowl, combine the couscous and the water. Let stand until all the water is absorbed, 20 to 25 minutes. Set aside.

2 • Coarsely shred one of the carrots, one of the zucchini, and the onion. Set aside.

3 • With a vegetable peeler, make long, thin ribbons from the remaining carrots and zucchini. Set aside.

4 • Separate the broccoli into small florets. Set aside.

5 • In a medium skillet over medium-high heat, warm 2 tablespoons of the olive oil and half of the curry powder. Stir continuously until the oil foams and gives off a pleasant aroma, 30 to 40 seconds. Add the walnuts. Cook, stirring, until they turn a light golden color, 1 minute. With a slotted spoon, transfer them to a small bowl. Set aside.

6 • To the skillet, add the shredded vegetables and the garlic. Stir occasionally until the carrots are tender, 4 to 5 minutes.

7 • In a large bowl, combine the cooked vegetables with the couscous, eggs, flour, ¼ cup of the cream, the walnut pieces, and half of the salt and pepper. Set aside.

(continued)

8 • Wipe out skillet and add remaining tablespoon of oil. Over medium-high heat, warm the remaining curry powder, stirring continuously, until it gives off a pleasant aroma, 30 to 40 seconds. Add the carrot and zucchini ribbons, and the broccoli florets. Cook, stirring occasionally, until the carrots are tender, 3 to 4 minutes. Reduce the heat to medium-low. Add the remaining cream, salt, and pepper. Cook until the sauce thickens somewhat, 10 to 12 minutes.

9 • Meanwhile, cook the croquettes. In another medium skillet over medium-high heat, pour vegetable oil to a depth of ½ inch. Heat until a pinch of the couscous mixture dropped into it sizzles instantly. Place ⅛ cup of the couscous mixture into the skillet. With a spatula, flatten into a croquette 2 to 2½ inches in diameter. Fry until golden brown, 3 to 4 minutes on each side. Transfer to a plate lined with paper towels to drain. Proceed in this manner until all of the couscous mixture is used.

10 • Spoon some of the cream onto each of 6 warm dinner plates. Place 3 overlapping croquettes in the center. Top with equal amounts of the creamed vegetables, and serve.

TOGOLESE COUSCOUS IN PEANUT SAUCE

Couscous Azindessi, also called couscous Mafé, *is part of the culinary heritage of several West African nations, including Mali, Ivory Coast, Senegal, and Togo. Geneviève Béké, an accomplished Togolese* cuisinière, *prefers baking couscous in her oven rather than cooking it on top of the stove.*

Serves 4

3 garlic cloves, minced
1 chicken bouillon cube, crushed
½ teaspoon ground ginger
¼ teaspoon freshly ground pepper
1 pound chicken legs and thighs
1 large tomato, peeled, seeded (see page 22),
    and coarsely chopped
1 medium onion, coarsely chopped
2⅓ cups chicken broth
3 tablespoons peanut oil
1 tablespoon tomato paste with roasted garlic
4 tablespoons smooth peanut butter
1 teaspoon salt
1 cup couscous
½ cup (about 4 ounces) salted,
    dry-roasted peanuts, crushed
4 green onions, thinly sliced, for garnish

1 • In a large bowl, mix the garlic, crushed bouillon cube, ground ginger, and pepper. Coat the chicken with this mixture. Set aside.

2 • In a blender, combine the tomato, onion, and 1 cup of the chicken broth. Blend until fairly smooth. Set aside.

3 • In a heavy, medium casserole over medium-high heat, warm 2 tablespoons of the oil. Cook the chicken, turning with tongs until browned on all sides. Add the tomato-onion-broth mixture. Cook, covered, until the sauce comes to a low boil, about 5 minutes. Stir in the tomato paste and peanut butter. Reduce heat to medium. Continue cooking, covered, until the chicken is tender, 40 to 45 minutes. Dilute the sauce with a little water or broth if it becomes too thick. Season with half of the salt.

4 • Meanwhile, heat the oven to 325 degrees F. Pour the couscous into a 9-by-13-inch baking dish. In a medium saucepan over medium-high heat, bring the remaining chicken broth, the salt, and the remaining oil to a boil. Pour over the couscous. Stir once. Cover tightly with foil and bake until the couscous is tender, 12 to 15 minutes. Remove it from the oven, and fluff it with a fork. Stir in the peanuts. Mound the couscous in the center of a warm shallow serving platter. Surround with the chicken and top with the peanut sauce. Garnish with the chopped green onions and serve.

COUSCOUS WITH LENTILS
AND CRISPY ONION RINGS

I have adapted this dish from a popular Middle Eastern lentil and rice pilaf called mujjadarah. *Serve it hot or at room temperature.*

Serves 4

3 large onions
4 tablespoons olive oil
1½ cups water
¼ cup green, *du Puy* French lentils, rinsed and drained
1 bay leaf
½ cup couscous
½ cup plus 3 tablespoons beef broth
¾ teaspoon salt
1 tablespoon flour
Vegetable oil for frying
Freshly ground pepper to taste

1 • Cut 1 of the onions into ⅛-inch-thick slices. Separate the slices into rings. Set aside on paper towels to dry.

2 • Finely dice the 2 remaining onions. In a large skillet over medium heat, heat 2 tablespoons of the olive oil. Cook the diced onions, stirring occasionally, until they turn a deep, caramel color, 40 to 45 minutes. Set aside.

3 • Meanwhile, in a medium saucepan, combine the water, lentils, and bay leaf. Cover, and cook over medium heat until the lentils are tender, 15 to 20 minutes. Discard the bay leaf. Drain and set aside.

4 • In another medium saucepan over medium heat, warm the remaining olive oil. Add the couscous. Cook, stirring, until it gives off a pleasant, toasted aroma, 2 to 3 minutes. Add the broth and ½ teaspoon of the salt. Stir once. Remove from the heat. Cover and let stand until the couscous is tender, 12 to 15 minutes.

5 • In a paper or plastic bag, combine the sliced onions with the flour. Shake to coat. In a medium saucepan or deep-fat fryer, heat the vegetable oil to the smoking stage. Fry the rings until they turn crispy and golden brown, 1½ to 2 minutes. Using a slotted spoon, transfer to a plate lined with paper towels to drain. Set aside.

6 • Add the lentils and the couscous to the diced onions in the skillet. Season with the remaining salt and the pepper. Stir to blend. Cook until heated through. Transfer to a warm serving platter. Top with the crispy onion rings, and serve.

SHREDDED PORK COUSCOUS TAMALES WITH TOMATILLO SAUCE

Making tamales can be time-consuming. For this reason, I sometimes assemble my tamales a few days ahead and freeze them. Count on 2 tamales per person for an appetizer; 4 for a main course.

Serves 6 (makes about 2 dozen tamales)

32 corn husks (see Note)

FILLING

1 pound pork butt, cut into 2-inch chunks
4 garlic cloves
1½ teaspoons ground cumin
1 teaspoon oregano
⅛ teaspoon cinnamon
1 medium onion, diced
2 tablespoons tomato paste
¾ teaspoon Mexican pasilla chili powder
One 4-ounce jar diced red pimientos, drained
1½ teaspoons salt
2⅔ cups chicken broth
3 tablespoons vegetable oil
2 cups couscous
3 large eggs, well beaten

TOMATILLO SAUCE

12 fresh tomatillos, papery husks removed, quartered
⅔ cup chicken broth
One 4-ounce can diced green chiles, drained
2 garlic cloves, minced
40 sprigs fresh cilantro
½ teaspoon chili powder
1½ teaspoons salt
2 drops Tabasco sauce (optional)

1 • Immerse the corn husks in a large pot of boiling water. Remove from the heat, and let stand until soft and pliable, 40 to 45 minutes. Drain the husks and pat dry. Reserve 3 or 4 husks to line a steamer basket or colander. With kitchen scissors, cut 2 of the husks lengthwise into ¼-inch strips. Set aside.

2 • To make the filling: Heat the oven to 375 degrees F. In a medium, heavy roasting pan, place the pork, garlic, cumin, oregano, cinnamon, and ½ cup of water. Cover tightly. Bake until the meat is very tender, 1½ to 2 hours. With a slotted spoon, transfer the meat to a bowl and let cool somewhat. Using 2 forks, shred the meat. Set aside. Reserve 2 tablespoons of the pan juices.

3 • In a medium skillet over medium-high heat, combine the reserved pan juices with the onion, tomato paste, and chili powder. Cook, stirring occasionally, until the onion is tender, 3 to 4 minutes. Add the pimientos, shredded pork, and ½ teaspoon of the salt. Stir to blend. Set aside to cool.

4 • In a large saucepan, bring the broth, the remaining salt, and the vegetable oil to a boil. Add the couscous in a stream. Stir once. Remove from the heat. Cover and let stand until the couscous is tender, 12 to 15 minutes. Transfer to a large bowl and let cool. Combine the couscous with the eggs. Mix well. Set aside.

5 • **To assemble the tamales:** Open a husk and position it so the long edge faces you. Place ¼ cup of the couscous mixture in the center of the husk. With your fingers, flatten the couscous to form a 3-by-3-inch square about ¼ inch thick. Spread a heaping tablespoon of the meat mixture in the center of this square, leaving a 1-inch border of uncovered couscous top and bottom, and ½ inch on the sides. Grasp the bottom edge of the husk and fold it in half lengthwise. Compress to seal the couscous to itself and enclose the meat filling. Gently unfold the husk, then wrap it around the couscous, as you would an egg roll. Fold over the tapered end, and tie it with a reserved precut strip of husk. Compress the other end and leave untied. Proceed in this manner for all the tamales.

6 • Line the bottom of a steamer basket or colander with the reserved husks. Set the tamales upright, tied end down, inside the steamer basket. Bring water to a boil in bottom part of the steamer. Cover tightly. Steam the tamales until firm and heated through, 40 to 45 minutes.

7 • **To make the tomatillo sauce:** In a medium saucepan over medium-high heat, combine the tomatillos, chicken broth, green chiles, garlic, and half of the cilantro. Cook until the tomatillos are tender, 15 to 20 minutes. Remove from the heat and let cool. Transfer the sauce to a blender and purée. Strain the sauce through a medium-meshed sieve and return the sauce to the pan. Stir in the chili powder and salt. Keep warm until serving time. Add the remaining cilantro, and the Tabasco, if using, before serving.

8 • Place a steamed tamal in its husk on a heated dinner plate. With kitchen scissors, cut away a large, V-shaped piece of husk to expose the couscous. Spoon a generous amount of tomatillo sauce over and around each tamale, and serve.

NOTE: *To obtain uniform, high-quality corn husks, see Sources on page 116.*

BAKED ONIONS FILLED WITH COUSCOUS AND PRESERVED LEMON

Preserved lemons are the quintessential Moroccan condiment, for which there is no substitute. You will have to prepare them several weeks ahead of time. It will be worth the wait.

Serves 4

4 large red onions (8 to 12 ounces each)
4 tablespoons olive oil
1 medium carrot, peeled and finely diced
4 ounces cooked, diced beef
3 tablespoons Worcestershire sauce
1½ teaspoons salt
¼ teaspoon freshly ground pepper
1⅔ cups beef broth
½ cup couscous
2 tablespoons butter
40 sprigs parsley, finely chopped (about 4 tablespoons)
1 tablespoon Moroccan Preserved Lemon rind
   (see page 23)
2 eggs, lightly beaten
Fresh parsley for garnish

1 • Peel the onions. Slice a dime-size piece from the root end to create a flat base. With a melon baller, scoop out the inside, leaving a shell ¼ inch thick. (If you accidentally perforate the base, patch it with a piece of onion.) Proceed in the same manner for the remaining onions. Set aside. Transfer the pieces of onion to a cutting board, and finely chop.

2 • Place the shells in a large saucepan filled with lightly salted water, over medium-high heat. Cook, covered, for 10 minutes. Drain and set aside to cool.

3 • In a large skillet over medium-high heat, warm 2 tablespoons of olive oil. Add half of the chopped onion, the diced carrot, beef, and Worcestershire sauce. Cook, stirring occasionally, until the carrot is browned, 15 to 20 minutes. Season with half of the salt and pepper. Set aside.

4 • In a small saucepan, bring ⅔ cup of the broth and the remaining salt and pepper to a boil. Add the couscous in a stream. Stir once. Remove from the heat. Cover and let stand until the couscous is tender, 12 to 15 minutes. In a medium bowl, combine the couscous with the cooked vegetables, butter, parsley, preserved lemon rind, and eggs. Set aside.

5 • Preheat the oven to 425 degrees F. Spread the remaining chopped onions on the bottom of an 8-by-8-inch baking dish that can go from oven to table. Set the onion shells in the dish. Fill each one with equal portions of the couscous mixture. Drizzle with the remaining 2 tablespoons of olive oil. Spoon the remaining cup of broth over and around the onions. Cover, first with foil, then with a lid. Bake until the onions are tender, 50 to 55 minutes. Uncover. Spoon some of the sauce over the onions, garnish with parsley, and serve.

COCONUT MILK COUSCOUS CURRY
WITH SEARED SCALLOPS

In India and Southeast Asia, there are as many recipes for curry powder as there are cooks. For this dish, I use a sweet (mild) curry blend containing turmeric, Moroccan coriander, cumin, ginger, nutmeg, fennel, cinnamon, fenugreek, white pepper, arrowroot, cardamom, cloves, black peppercorns, and red pepper. Add piquancy to taste by serving hot sauce on the side.

Serves 6

¾ cup water
½ **extra large fish-flavored bouillon cube** (see Note)
2 tablespoons peanut oil
½ **teaspoon salt**
⅔ **cup couscous**
20 sprigs fresh cilantro, chopped (about 2 tablespoons)
3 green onions, white parts only, finely chopped
2 teaspoons minced gingerroot
2 garlic cloves, minced
1 teaspoon sweet (mild) curry powder (see Note)
18 jumbo scallops, rinsed, drained, and patted dry
1 cup coconut milk (see Note)
½ **cup salted, dry-roasted cashews, chopped**
Fresh cilantro leaves for garnish
Indonesian *sambal manis* or Thai hot sauce
(optional, see Note)

1 • In a medium saucepan, bring the water, half a bouillon cube, 1 tablespoon of the oil, and the salt to a boil. Add the couscous in a stream. Stir once. Remove from the heat. Cover and let stand until the couscous is tender, 12 to 15 minutes. Combine with the cilantro and green onions. Keep warm.

2 • Meanwhile, in a medium, nonstick skillet over medium-high heat, warm the remaining oil, the gingerroot, garlic, and curry powder. Cook, stirring, until the foaming subsides, 30 to 40 seconds. Add the scallops, searing them until they are no longer opaque, 2 to 3 minutes on each side. Add the coconut milk. Stir, scraping the bottom of the pan to remove charred bits, 30 to 40 seconds. Remove from the heat.

3 • Gently pack equal amounts of couscous into 6 generously greased 6-ounce ramekins. Unmold into the centers of 6 warm dinner plates. Arrange three scallops on each plate around the base of the couscous. Spoon the sauce over and around the couscous. Garnish with cashews and cilantro leaves. Serve with hot sauce on the side, if using.

NOTE: *Sambal manis, Thai hot sauce, fish bouillon cubes, and cans of coconut milk are available in Asian markets and in the Asian section of large supermarkets. For a source of freshly blended sweet (mild) and hot curry powders, see Sources, page 116.*

COUSCOUS QUENELLES FLORENTINE

The French word quenelle *is derived from the German* knodel, *meaning "dumpling." You can prepare and steam* quenelles *a day ahead and refrigerate them until you're ready to bake.*

Serves 6

¾ cup broth
1½ teaspoons salt
¾ cup couscous
½ cup water
One 10-ounce package frozen chopped spinach
½ teaspoon freshly ground pepper
6 tablespoons butter, softened
2 eggs, lightly beaten
¾ teaspoon nutmeg
¼ cup flour
2 cups milk, heated
½ cup half-and-half or light cream, heated
1 cup (about 4 ounces) grated Gruyère cheese

1 • In a medium saucepan, bring the broth and half of the salt to a boil. Add the couscous in a stream. Stir once. Remove from the heat. Cover and let stand until the couscous is tender, 12 to 15 minutes.

2 • Meanwhile, in a medium saucepan over medium-high heat, bring the water to a boil. Add the spinach and cook until tender, 8 to 10 minutes. Drain in a sieve or colander, pressing with the back of a large spoon to squeeze out as much liquid as possible. Set aside.

3 • In a medium metal bowl, using your hands, thoroughly blend the couscous, half of the pepper, 2 tablespoons of the butter, the eggs, half of the nutmeg, and the drained spinach. Pat the cous-cous mixture in a ¼-inch layer on the bottom and sides of the bowl. Refrigerate until it becomes puttylike, about 1 hour.

4 • Using your hands, fashion 1 heaping table-spoon of the couscous mixture into a plump "sausage" 2 inches long by ¾ inch in diameter. Proceed in this manner until all the couscous mixture is used. Refrigerate until ready to steam.

5 • Place the *quenelles* in the top part of a lightly oiled *couscoussier*, a steamer, or a colander set over a pot of boiling water. Cook, covered, until the *quenelles* are firm, 15 to 20 minutes.

6 • Preheat the oven to 425 degrees F. In a medium saucepan, melt the remaining butter over medium-high heat. Whisk in the flour, and cook until the mixture thickens, 4 to 5 minutes. Add the warmed milk and half-and-half, whisking until lumps disappear and the sauce thickens, 6 to 8 minutes. Add the remaining nutmeg, salt, and pepper, and the cheese. Cook, stirring, until the cheese melts, 4 to 5 minutes. Set aside.

7 • Spread some of the cheese sauce on the bottom of a medium baking dish. Set the *quenelles* in a single layer in the dish. Cover with the remaining cheese sauce. Bake until bubbly and brown, 12 to 15 minutes. Serve immediately.

DESSERTS

CHOCOLATE-AMARETTO COUSCOUS TRUFFLES

Chocolate truffle purists might wonder at this unusual chocolate-couscous combination, until they take their first bite. Couscous lends a distinctive textural nuance to this nontraditional confection. The truffles will keep for several days in a covered container in the refrigerator. Roll the truffles in the ground almonds just before serving so the nuts don't lose their crunch.

Makes about thirty 1-inch truffles

5¾ cups plus 2 tablespoons water

⅔ cup couscous

4½ ounces semisweet chocolate

3 tablespoons amaretto (almond liqueur)

1 teaspoon almond extract

⅓ cup (4 ounces) almond paste,
 at room temperature

5 tablespoons butter, at room temperature

1 cup (about 3½ ounces) slivered almonds,
 toasted (see page 20), and coarsely ground

1 tablespoon cocoa powder, sifted (optional)

2 tablespoons confectioners' sugar (optional)

1 • In a medium saucepan, bring ¾ cup plus 2 tablespoons of water to a boil. Add the couscous in a stream. Stir once. Remove from heat. Cover and let stand until couscous is tender, 12 to 15 minutes. Set aside.

2 • Place the chocolate, amaretto, and almond extract in a medium, heat-proof bowl. Set aside.

3 • In a large heavy skillet over medium-high heat, bring the remaining 5 cups of water just to the point of simmering. Remove the skillet from the heat. Place the bowl filled with the chocolate mixture in the hot water bath, stirring occasionally, until the chocolate is melted. Set aside.

4 • Meanwhile, in a small bowl, thoroughly blend the almond paste with the butter. Add this to the chocolate mixture and stir until smooth. Add the couscous and mix thoroughly. Refrigerate until the mixture achieves a puttylike consistency, 30 to 45 minutes.

5 • To make the truffles, fashion 1 level tablespoon of the chocolate-couscous mixture into a ball 1 inch in diameter. Continue in this manner until all the mixture is used. Refrigerate in a tightly covered container.

6 • Thirty minutes before serving, remove the truffles from the refrigerator. Roll them in ground almonds to coat. Serve in fluted paper cups. (For cocoa-covered truffles, see Note below.)

NOTE: *To coat the truffles with cocoa, sift 1 tablespoon cocoa powder with 2 tablespoons confectioners' sugar into a shallow bowl. Blend until uniform in color. Roll the truffles in the cocoa mixture and refrigerate. Their color will deepen as the cocoa powder is absorbed into the surface of the truffle. Store in a tightly covered container in the refrigerator. Take them out 30 minutes before serving.*

RASPBERRY COUSCOUS TRIFLE

Once you try the couscous version of this traditional English dessert, you may never prepare it with pound cake again!

Serves 8

COUSCOUS
2/3 cup water
1/4 teaspoon salt
1 tablespoon butter
1/2 cup couscous
2 tablespoons sugar
2 tablespoons amaretto (almond liqueur)

CUSTARD
1/3 cup sugar
3 tablespoons cornstarch
1/8 teaspoon salt
2 1/2 cups milk
2 egg yolks, lightly beaten
2 teaspoons vanilla extract

COULIS
One 12-ounce package frozen raspberries, thawed
1/2 cup water
1/3 cup plus 2 tablespoons sugar
1 cup heavy (whipping) cream, chilled
1 teaspoon vanilla extract
Two 6-ounce boxes fresh raspberries
Fresh mint leaves for garnish

1 • To make the couscous: In a medium saucepan over medium heat, bring the water, salt, and butter to a boil. Remove from the heat. Add the couscous in a stream. Stir once. Cover and let stand until couscous is tender, 12 to 15 minutes. Transfer to a bowl and stir in the sugar and amaretto. Set aside.

2 • To make the custard: In a medium saucepan over medium heat, combine the sugar, cornstarch, and salt. Add the milk, and whisk continuously until the mixture is warm. With a measuring cup, remove 1/4 cup of the mixture, and blend with the egg yolks. Return this egg mixture to the saucepan. Whisk continuously until bubbles form and the custard begins to thicken, 5 to 6 minutes. Remove the custard from the heat, and stir in the vanilla. Immediately combine 1/3 cup of the hot custard with the couscous. Spoon equal portions of this couscous mixture into eight 6-ounce clear parfait glasses or small bowls. Spoon equal amounts of the remaining hot custard over each dessert. Set aside.

3 • To make the coulis: In a blender or food processor, purée the thawed raspberries with the water. Strain into a medium saucepan. Over medium heat, combine 1/3 cup of the sugar with the strained purée. Cook, stirring occasionally, until the mixture reduces by a quarter, 5 to 6 minutes. Spoon equal amounts of coulis over the custard in each parfait glass.

4 • In a chilled metal bowl, whip the cream until soft peaks form. With a spatula, gently fold in the vanilla and the remaining sugar. Reserve 8 fresh raspberries. Arrange the remaining raspberries on top of the coulis in each parfait glass. Top with a generous dollop of whipped cream. Garnish with reserved berries and mint leaves, and serve.

COUSCOUS MANGO MOUSSE

Sweet and fragrant tropical mangoes are available almost year-round in the United States, thanks to growers in Florida, California, Mexico, and Central and South America. This dessert is a wonderful way to savor one of the world's most popular fruits.

Serves 6

1 cup water

¾ cup couscous

4 tablespoons sugar

2 juice oranges, preferably Valencia

2 tablespoons Cointreau or other
  orange-flavored liqueur

1 ripe mango (about 1¼ pounds)

1 cup heavy (whipping) cream, chilled

1 teaspoon vanilla extract

One 8-ounce container vanilla yogurt

1 • In a medium saucepan over medium-high heat, bring the water to a boil. Add the couscous in a stream. Stir once. Remove from the heat. Cover and let stand until the couscous is tender, 12 to 15 minutes. Mix in 2 tablespoons of the sugar. Cover tightly and set aside.

2 • Scrub one of the oranges under running water and pat dry. With a vegetable peeler, remove the zest, being careful not to peel away any of the white pith. Finely mince the zest. Set aside.

3 • Squeeze the oranges to obtain about ¾ cup of juice. Strain through a medium-meshed sieve into a small saucepan. Over medium heat, boil down the juice until it has reduced to about 2 table-spoons, and has the consistency of molten honey, 4 to 5 minutes. Stir in the Cointreau. Set aside.

4 • Peel the mango and cut the flesh away from the seed. Cut half into thin wedges and coarsely dice the rest. Set aside.

5 • In a chilled metal bowl, whip the cream until soft peaks form. Fold in the vanilla and the remaining sugar. Refrigerate 1 cup of the whipped cream for serving. In a medium bowl, combine the rest of the whipped cream with the yogurt and the diced mango. Refrigerate.

6 • Before serving, combine the yogurt-mango mixture with the couscous. Spoon equal amounts into 6 parfait glasses or small bowls. Top each dessert with a generous dollop of the reserved whipped cream and mango wedges. Drizzle with orange-Cointreau sauce, sprinkle with minced orange zest, and serve.

COUSCOUS PUMPKIN FLAN
WITH GRAPE "HONEY"

Grape "honey" is a condiment that has been used by the Semitic peoples of the eastern Mediterranean for thousands of years. It adds a delicate and natural sweetness to this unusual flan.

Serves 8

1 pound pumpkin or butternut squash,
  cut into large chunks
1¼ cups water
½ teaspoon salt
1 tablespoon butter
⅔ cup couscous
½ cup evaporated milk, scalded
2 eggs, lightly beaten
1 cup tightly packed golden brown sugar
½ teaspoon ground cloves
½ teaspoon ground nutmeg
1 teaspoon ground ginger
1 teaspoon ground cinnamon
2 cups unsweetened grape juice
1 pint heavy (whipping) cream, chilled
¼ cup granulated sugar
2 teaspoons vanilla

1 • Preheat the oven to 375 degrees F. Place the pumpkin in an ovenproof dish and bake until tender, 50 to 55 minutes. Let cool and peel. In a blender or food processor, purée the pumpkin. Set aside 1 cup of the purée and store the rest for another use.

2 • In a medium saucepan over medium-high heat, bring 1 cup of the water, the salt, and butter to a boil. Add the couscous in a stream. Stir once.

Remove from the heat. Cover and let stand until the couscous is tender, 12 to 15 minutes. Set aside.

3 • In a medium bowl combine the couscous with the pumpkin purée, milk, remaining ¼ cup of water, the eggs, brown sugar, ground cloves, nutmeg, ginger, and cinnamon. Pour into a straight-sided, lightly oiled, nonstick, 9-inch pie pan. Cover tightly with aluminum foil. Set the pan in a steamer basket or on a trivet placed in a large, deep pan of lightly simmering water. Water should barely touch the base of the pie pan. Cover the large pan with a lid. Steam until the flan is firm, about 1½ hours.

4 • Meanwhile, pour the grape juice into a medium, nonreactive saucepan over medium heat. Cook until the juice reduces to about ⅓ cup. This will take about 25 to 30 minutes.

5 • Remove flan from the water bath. Unmold onto a warm serving platter.

6 • Pour the grape "honey" over and around the flan. Set aside.

7 • In a chilled metal bowl, whip the heavy cream until soft peaks form. Fold in the sugar and the vanilla. Cut the flan into pie-shaped wedges, and serve with generous dollops of whipped cream.

PINEAPPLE-BANANA COUSCOUS TAMALES WITH COCONUT-CREAM TOPPING

The inspiration for this recipe was an ambrosial pineapple tamale I tasted while serving as a food judge at the annual Indio International Tamale Festival, in California's Coachella Valley. Here, of course, I substitute couscous for traditional Mexican masa.

Serves 12 (makes about 2 dozen tamales)

32 corn husks (see Note)
2²/₃ cups water
1 teaspoon salt
6 tablespoons butter
2 cups couscous
¾ cup coconut cream (see Note)
4 medium bananas
¼ cup tightly packed dark brown sugar
1½ cups dried candied pineapple chunks
½ teaspoon ground cinnamon, plus extra for garnish
3 tablespoons rum
1 cup heavy (whipping) cream, chilled
1 teaspoon vanilla extract

1 • Immerse the corn husks in a large pot of boiling water. Remove from the heat, and let stand until soft and pliable, 40 to 45 minutes. Drain the husks and pat dry. Reserve 3 or 4 of the husks to line a steamer basket or colander. With kitchen scissors, cut 2 of the husks lengthwise into ¼-inch strips. Set aside.

2 • In a large saucepan, bring the water, salt, and 3 tablespoons of the butter to a boil. Add the couscous and ½ cup of the coconut cream. Stir to blend. Remove from the heat. Cover and let stand until the couscous is tender, 12 to 15 minutes. Transfer to a large bowl, and set aside.

3 • Quarter the bananas lengthwise, and cut into ¼-inch dice. In a skillet over medium-high heat, warm the remaining butter. Add the dark brown sugar. Cook, stirring, until the sugar melts, 1 to 2 minutes. Add the diced bananas. Stir to coat. Cook until the bananas soften somewhat, 2 to 3 minutes. Remove from the heat. Add the pineapple chunks, cinnamon, and rum. Stir to blend. Set aside.

4 • To assemble the tamales, position a husk so the long edge faces you. Place ¼ cup of the couscous mixture in the center. With a spatula, flatten the couscous to form a 3-by-3-inch square about ¼ inch thick. Set a heaping tablespoon of the pineapple-banana mixture in the center of this square, and form into a sausage shape. Leave a 1-inch border of uncovered couscous top and bottom, and ½ inch on the sides. Grasp the bottom edge of the husk and fold it in half lengthwise. Compress to seal the couscous to itself and enclose the filling. Gently unfold the husk, then wrap it around the couscous, as you would an egg roll. Fold over the tapered end, and tie with a reserved precut strip of husk. Compress the other end but leave untied. Proceed in this manner until all the tamales are assembled.

(continued)

5 • Line the bottom of a steamer basket or colander with the reserved husks. Set the tamales upright, closed end down, inside the colander. Bring water to a boil in bottom part of the steamer. Cover tightly. Steam the tamales until firm and heated through, 40 to 45 minutes.

6 • In a chilled metal bowl, whip the cream until soft peaks form. Fold in the vanilla and remaining coconut cream. Set aside.

7 • Place a steamed tamal in its husk on a dessert plate. With kitchen scissors, cut away a large, V-shaped piece of husk to expose the couscous. Spoon a generous dollop of coconut cream sauce on or near the tamal, sprinkle with cinnamon, and serve.

NOTE: *Cans of coconut cream are available in liquor stores or Asian markets. To obtain uniform, high-quality corn husks, see Sources on page 116.*

COUSCOUS À L'ORANGE
WITH ALMONDS AND DATES

Couscous à l'Orange marries the flavors of Greek baklava and the Moroccan sweet couscous called s'ffa.

Serves 8

10 juice oranges, preferably Valencia
1 tablespoon orange blossom water (see Note)
½ teaspoon salt
1 cup couscous
½ cup honey
4 tablespoons butter
1½ cups (about 6 ounces) slivered almonds,
   toasted (see page 20), and coarsely chopped
16 medium dates, pitted and coarsely chopped
Ground cinnamon for garnish
Fresh mint leaves for garnish

1 • Scrub 2 or 3 of the oranges under running water and pat dry. With a vegetable peeler, remove the zest, being careful not to peel away any of the white pith. Finely mince to obtain about ½ cup. Squeeze and strain the juice from the zested oranges and 2 of the others, to obtain 1⅓ cups juice. Set aside.

2 • With a sharp knife, peel the remaining oranges, removing all the white pith. Separate the oranges into sections. Remove the membranes and seeds. Transfer to a small bowl and add the orange blossom water. Mix gently and set aside.

3 • In a small saucepan over medium heat, bring the reserved orange juice and salt to a boil. Add the couscous in a stream. Stir once. Remove from the heat. Cover and let stand until the couscous is tender, 15 to 20 minutes.

4 • In another small saucepan over low heat, warm the honey. Remove from the heat and add the butter, stirring, until it has melted. Add the honey-butter mixture to the couscous, along with the orange zest and 1 cup of the chopped almonds. Mix thoroughly. Spoon ½ cup of this mixture into 8 small ramekins or bowls. Top with chopped dates. Pat down evenly. Cover and set aside at room temperature.

5 • To facilitate unmolding, 10 minutes before serving, set the ramekins in a pan of hot water (the water should come halfway up the sides of the ramekins). Invert ramekins onto individual dessert plates. Arrange the orange sections in a pinwheel pattern around the couscous. Garnish with the reserved almonds, a dash of cinnamon, and a mint leaf, and serve.

NOTE: *Orange blossom water is available in Middle Eastern markets and in some liquor stores.*

sources

R.W. GREGORY CO.
P.O. Drawer 795127
Dallas, TX 75379
(888) 794-4875
Corn husks. Minimum order: 1 carton.

MELISSA'S WORLD VARIETY PRODUCE
P.O. Box 21127
Los Angeles, CA 90021
(800) 468-7111
www.melissas.com
Sun-dried tomatoes, dried mushrooms, and spices.

NOMADS OF SANTA FE
207 Shelby Street
Santa Fe, NM 87501
(800) 360-4807
www.nomads-santafe.com
Couscoussiers.

THE SPICE HOUSE
1941 Central Street
Evanston, IL 60201
(847) 328-3711
www.thespicehouse.com
Spices.

SUR LA TABLE
1765 Sixth Avenue South
Seattle, WA 98134
(800) 243-0852
Wide selection of cookware, including *couscoussiers.*

bibliography

Bloom, Carole. *The International Dictionary of Desserts, Pastries, and Confections*. New York: Hearst Books, 1995.

Dagher, Shawky M., ed. "Traditional Foods in the Near East." Food and Nutrition paper no. 50. Food and Agriculture Organization of the United Nations, 1991.

Facciola, Stephen. *Cornucopia II: A Sourcebook of Edible Plants*. Vista, CA: Kampong Publications, 1998.

Lakhal, Naima. "La production et la consommation de couscous au Maroc: De l'artisanat à l'industrie." Ph.D. diss., University of Toulouse Le Mirail, 1988. Available from the author at B.P. 83, El Jadida Principale, Morocco.

McGee, Harold. *On Food and Cooking: The Science and Lore of the Kitchen*. New York: Macmillan Publishing Co., 1984.

Morse, Kitty. *A Biblical Feast: Foods from the Holy Land*. Berkeley: Ten Speed Press, 1998.
—— *Come with Me to the Kasbah: A Cook's Tour of Morocco*. Casablanca: SERAR, 1989.
—— *Cooking at the Kasbah: Recipes from My Moroccan Kitchen*. San Francisco: Chronicle Books, 1998.
—— *The Vegetarian Table: North Africa*. San Francisco: Chronicle Books, 1996.

Morsy, Magali. *Le Monde des couscous*. Aix-en-Provence: Edisud, 1996.

Noakes, Greg, and Laidia Chouat-Noakes. "Couscous. The Measure of the Maghrib." *Aramco World* magazine: November–December 1998, 16–24.

Perry, Charles. "A Funny Thing Happened on the Way to the Noodle Shop," *The Los Angeles Times*, Thursday, 21 April 1994.
—— "Couscous and its Cousins." In *Proceedings of the Oxford Symposium on Food and Cookery*, 1989, 176–177. Prospect Books, 1990.

Toussaint-Samat, Maguelonne. *Histoire gourmande des grands plats: Couscous*. Tournai (Belgium): Casterman, 1994.

Wright, Clifford. *A Mediterreanean Feast: The Story of the Birth of the Celebrated Cuisines of the Mediterranean from the Merchants of Venice to the Barbary Corsairs, Illustrated with More than 500 Recipes*. New York: William Morrow and Co., 1999.
—— *Cucina Paradiso: The Heavenly Food of Sicily*. New York: Simon and Schuster, 1992.
—— "Cuscusù: A Paradigm of Arab-Sicilian Cuisine." *The Journal of Gastronomy 5, No. 4* (Spring 1990), 19–37.

index

table of equivalents

THE EXACT EQUIVALENTS IN THE FOLLOWING TABLES HAVE BEEN ROUNDED FOR CONVENIENCE.

LIQUID/DRY MEASURES

U.S.	METRIC
¼ teaspoon	1.25 milliliters
½ teaspoon	2.5 milliliters
1 teaspoon	5 milliliters
1 tablespoon (3 teaspoons)	15 milliliters
1 fluid ounce (2 tablespoons)	30 milliliters
¼ cup	60 milliliters
⅓ cup	80 milliliters
½ cup	120 milliliters
1 cup	240 milliliters
1 pint (2 cups)	480 milliliters
1 quart (4 cups, 32 ounces)	960 milliliters
1 gallon (4 quarts)	3.84 liters
1 ounce (by weight)	28 grams
1 pound	454 grams
2.2 pounds	1 kilogram

LENGTH

U.S.	METRIC
⅛ inch	3 millimeters
¼ inch	6 millimeters
½ inch	12 millimeters
1 inch	2.5 centimeters

OVEN TEMPERATURE

FAHRENHEIT	CELSIUS	GAS
250	120	½
275	140	1
300	150	2
325	160	3
350	180	4
375	190	5
400	200	6
425	220	7
450	230	8
475	240	9
500	260	10